HIDDEN TIBET

Roger Hicks is a freelance writer and photographer. Born in Cornwall in 1950, he has been interested in Tibet and the Tibetan culture since the age of seven. He has written numerous books on photography and, together with Ngakpa Chögyam, he is the author of *Great Ocean*, the authorised biography of the Dalai Lama, published by Element Books in 1984.

Frontispiece *Refugees are still coming out of Tibet. Many have been told that the Dalai Lama is dead, and when they see him – even for a few seconds at a public* darshan *– it is the greatest day of their lives. He always tries to spend a moment or two longer with the very young and the very old, and with new refugees.*

HIDDEN TIBET

The Land and Its People

ROGER HICKS

 Element Books

© Roger Hicks 1988

First published 1988 by
Element Books Limited
Longmead, Shaftesbury, Dorset

Printed and bound by Butler & Tanner Ltd.
Frome, Somerset

Designed by Humphrey Stone

British Library Cataloguing in Publication Data
Hicks, Roger
    Hidden Tibet
    1. Tibet (China) – History
    I. Title
    951'.5   DS786

ISBN 1-85230-030-2

CONTENTS

FOREWORD   vi

PREFACE   viii

ACKNOWLEDGEMENTS   x

BARDO   1

OLD TIBET   31

OCCUPIED TIBET   63

A WORLD IN EXILE   91

GLOSSARY   146

POSTSCRIPT – PHOTOGRAPHY   147

PHOTO CREDITS   148

FOREWORD

Mr Roger Hicks has done such a complete job with this book that there is hardly anything left to be said except to thank him and his wife, Frances – who also played no small part in its production – and all the others, too many to be named, who helped us at every stage of the work. Had it not been for their help and co-operation you would not be reading this book.

Roger has already dealt with the story of how we met and how we came to work on this book together. So I will not dwell on it at length here. But it needs to be said that if I had not met Roger when I did – it is unlikely that this book would have been ready now. The Information Office had plans to publish a pictorial book on Tibet with an accompanying text that would re-tell the story of our tragedy and suffering. We did not want to make any pretence at 'objectivity' as this word is now used or rather abused. The present trend – not only with politicians , but also with journalists, writers and scholars – is to take some information from both sides, mix the two together and then call it an 'objective' report or view-point – as the case may be.

What we wanted to do was to tell our side of the story as we experienced it and as we know it. But we did not want it to be charged with bitterness and clouded by emotion.

With over 1.2 million Tibetans dead in the short space of 35 years; more than 100,000 in exile scattered all over the world; an astounding monk population of over 600,000 at one time completely wiped out and now consisting of no more than a few hundred; 99 per cent of the monasteries and temples plundered and razed to the ground – some of them over a thousand years old – and with tens of thousands still languishing in prisons, concentration and labour camps, every Tibetan family has suffered as a result of the invasion and occupation of Tibet by Communist China and the national loss in terms of culture and religion alone is incalculable. In the face of such suffering and while we are still trying to gather together our scarred and broken lives, it is more than difficult to stick only to facts and leave aside our feelings and opinions. This is why we were looking for a non-Tibetan to write the text for us, a friend who knew our problems and understood our hopes and aspirations for a free and independent Tibet. And it is in Roger that we have found such a friend.

The Tibet that is past – a glimpse of which you will get through the pages of this book – we know, sadly, will never come again. But it is not to restore the past that we are struggling; though the loss is immense and painful. The whole purpose behind our struggle is that we should be left to govern our own lives. We do not seek anything beyond that. If the Chinese return to their country and leave us in our own, there is no reason for any trouble. Knowing this, our forefathers had clearly stated in the treaty of A.D. 821, signed between the Tibetan Emperor Ngadak Tri-Ralpachen and the T'ang dynasty to delineate the borders between Tibet and China, that – "Chinese are happy in China and Tibetans are happy in Tibet". His Holiness the Dalai Lama has also said time and again, "Our struggle is not anti-communist or anti-Chinese. It is not anti-revolution. It has nothing to do with race, or ideology. It is for the happiness of the six million Tibetans."

We hope that through the pages of this book more people will come to know about what has happened in Tibet since 1949 and to understand that the Tibetan people ask for no more than what all other people everywhere desire – to be left alone to lead their own lives in peace and harmony with the other nations of the world.

LODI G. GYARI
General Secretary (Addl.)
Information Office
Central Tibetan Secretariat
Dharamsala

PREFACE

This book grew out of another, the biography of His Holiness the Dalai Lama. From the beginning, I had wanted to do a picture book about Tibet and the Tibetan people in order to convey something of what has happened since the Chinese invasion in 1949-50. As a photographer, the visual richness of Tibetan culture fascinated me; as a writer, I felt that there was a need for someone to counter the endless propaganda put out by the Chinese; and purely personally, I felt that the Tibetan experience was something worth sharing. I did not want an academic or erudite book: I wanted something which conveyed the incredible warmth, friendliness, and coherence of Tibetan culture, and which showed how the Tibetan way of life has survived the most terrible assaults and survived into exile.

The biography was more than half completed when Gyari Rinpoche of the Information Office of His Holiness the Dalai Lama told me that his office had for some time been contemplating just such a book as I had in mind, and asked if I would be interested in working on it. I jumped at the chance. With the backing of the Tibetan Administration, the book would be very much easier to write; and as for the charge that I would be writing propaganda, I did not feel too worried about that. I already had a very clear idea of where I stood on the Tibetan question, and it was firmly on the side of the Tibetans. In any case, there was no need to lie or to distort the facts: the truth is persuasive enough.

The Great Thirteenth Dalai Lama wrote in his Political Testament that unless Tibet changed and modernised, the Land of Snows would be destroyed. In one way he has been proved only too right: the Chinese invaders have done their best to wipe out every vestige of Tibetan culture, and the old Tibet is gone forever. But many Tibetans agree that this is not necessarily a bad thing: a new Tibet can rise from the wreckage of the old. The destruction and rebirth may be agonising, but no one who has seen the progress which

Tibetans have made in exile can doubt the capacity of the Tibetan people for reconstruction. This book was written a quarter of a century after His Holiness the Dalai Lama escaped from Tibet with his life and little else; by the grace of the Three Jewels, perhaps another quarter-century will see him sitting once more on the Lion Throne.

R W H
Bristol and Dharamsala
1985

ACKNOWLEDGEMENTS

I had intended in these Acknowledgements to make separate thanks to those who supplied pictures, those who facilitated taking them, and those who either inspired the text or checked and read it. After beginning this task, I realised that the three were rarely separable; so many people were so helpful in so many ways that it would be impossible to thank them all.

Above all, I must thank His Holiness the Dalai Lama. He is an unending source of inspiration to the Tibetan people, and not only granted me several audiences and opportunities for photography but also loaned from his personal collection hitherto unpublished Kodachromes and other pictures taken before he left Tibet in 1959.

His younger brother Tendzin Choegyal (Ngari Rinpoche) was also extremely helpful, both in his official capacity as a member of the Private Office of His Holiness the Dalai Lama and personally, as a friend who provided deep insights into the Tibetan character; and I cannot mention Tendzin Choegyal without thanking also his wife, Rinchen Khando, and his colleague in the Private Office, Tempa Tsering. Rinchen Khando-la was again a warm friend, and Tempa-la's helpfulness, warmth, and dedication went far beyond the mere requirements of his post. Mrs Pema Gyalpo, His Holiness's sister, and all her staff at the Tibetan Children's Village schools in Dharamsala and Bylakuppe, allowed us almost unlimited access to the schools, and answered all our questions willingly and helpfully; Mrs Pema Gyalpo also loaned me some of her own photographic negatives to print. His Holiness's elder brother Lobsang Samten personally took me on a tour of the Tibetan Medical Institute, and introduced me to many of the staff and patients. The Great Thirteenth Dalai Lama said that he would have many brothers and sisters in his next life, in order to share his work: the *Yab-shi*, the 'Royal Family' of the Dalai Lama, certainly do this.

In the Information Office, Lodi Gyari Gyaltsen (Gyari Rinpoche) was the main begetter of this book; I am deeply grateful to him for giving me the opportunity to write it, as well as for arranging access to Tibetan settlements outside Dharamsala, including Bir, Bylakuppe, Chhauntra, and Hunsur. His colleague, Sonam Topgyal, was also instrumental in this. In the office itself, Lhasang Tsering could not have taken more care in checking the manuscript and verifying dates, facts, etc.; it is difficult to express my admiration for his thoroughness and of his command of the English language – though I must emphasise that any remaining mistakes are my own. Lobsang Tsultrim ('Uncle'), also of the Information Office, was also very helpful.

The Library of Tibetan Works and Archives was a valuable source of historical pictures, and I should particularly like to thank Gokhey Dekhang, the picture librarian, as well as the Director, Gyatso Tsering. Other historical pictures came from the Volkerkundermuseum, Zürich, for which I must thank Martin Brauen. Jamyang Norbu, former director of the Tibetan Institute of Performing Arts, loaned some very old negatives from a family collection, and Tsering Wangyal, the Editor of the *Tibetan Review*, supplied some more modern pictures. Pictures taken by members of the various Delegations came from the Kashag, where Tenzing Geyche was so helpful, and from the Offices of His Holiness the Dalai Lama in London and New York, where I would like to thank Phuntsog Wangyal and Tenzin Tethong respectively.

Before going on to thank those people who granted us access to other places, I must thank my wife, Frances Schultz, who is not only a very professional photographer in her own right, but also someone without whom I could not work. I must also thank Ngakpa Chögyam, my co-author of *Great Ocean*, an authorised biography of His Holiness the Dalai Lama, who introduced me to many people in Dharamsala and also took some of the pictures in this book, and his teacher, Lama Yeshi Dorje Rinpoche. Together or separately, Frances, Chögyam, and I photographed the places listed below: if I have not thanked individuals, it is simply because I did not have room to list everyone.

Bylakuppe settlement, south India: especial thanks to the head of the TCV school, and to Sonam Topgyal

Bir settlement, north India

Chhauntra Settlement, north India

Clement Town, Dehra Dun: especial thanks to Ngedon Gyatselling monastery and to Arnam Lama

Delek Hospital: all the staff were so helpful that it would be invidious to single out names

Hunsur settlement, south India: especial thanks to the Director, Norbu

Metalwork School, Dharamsala

Tibetan Institute of Performing Arts: especial thanks to Jamyang Norbu, the former Director

Tso.Pema (Rewalsar): thanks to all the monks of the Nyingma monastery and to Tsering Lama

Wood-carving and Thangka Painting Schools, LTWA: thanks to Gokhey Dekhang for arranging access

BARDO

After death, the body is taken by the *rtogs.lden* or body-breakers to a high place. It is customary for a few friends to attend, but not relatives: the sight is too harrowing. The body is broken into pieces while the vultures wait at a distance; once it is dismembered, the body-breakers withdraw and the vultures move in. After they have finished, even the bones are smashed and powdered. The destruction of the body is complete.

For seven times seven days, lamas and monks say prayers for the departed spirit. After death and the dissolution of the body, the spirit wanders in the between-life state, or *Bardo*. The visions it sees are described at length in the *Bardo Thodrol*, often known in the West as the 'Tibetan Book of the Dead'. Here are descriptions of fearsome monsters that live on human flesh, drink human blood, and dress in human skins and bones. But all the time, the Bardo Thodrol repeats that what is seen is illusion, and that if the spirit can recognise it

The rtogs.lden *break and rend the body for the vultures, and smash the bones when the flesh is gone.*

1

as such, he or she will be freed from the cycle of life and death, and go beyond duality. As the Great Mantra puts it,

> Om, gate, gate,
> Paragate,
> Parasamgate,
> Bodhi Sowha!

which may be translated thus:

> Gone, gone,
> Gone beyond
> Gone utterly beyond,
> What freedom!

But in the nature of things, most spirits fail to learn the nature of *shunyata* (voidness) when they are in the Bardo state, just as they failed to learn it when they were alive; and so, sometime in that seven times seven days, they will be drawn to a womb and take rebirth. Then, clad again in precious human form, or in any of the forms of the other realms, they have the chance to learn anew the lessons which they failed to learn in past lives.

Not all Tibetan religion is so dramatic; this magical cave shrine (location unknown) is typical of many in Tibet and in areas where the Tibetan cultural influence is strong.

Opposite Religious mendicants of many schools were common in Tibet; by feeding and housing them, ordinary people shared in the merit which they were accumulating; often, ordinary beggars would also carry religious symbols to improve their earnings.

2

Because we are more aware in the West of the religious aspects of Tibetan culture, it is easy to forget the secular side. This is a rich couple from Tsang, probably visiting Lhasa on pilgrimage, in traditional robes. The incredibly elaborate head-dress was characteristic of old Tibet, but is almost never seen in exile.

To draw a parallel between the Bardo state and the present state of Tibet may seem fanciful, and like all analogies it may be pursued too far. But the old Tibet is dead; the Chinese have done their best to break its body; and the spirit continues, so one day Tibet will be reborn. The spirit of Tibet lives in the six million Tibetans currently living under Chinese occupation, and in the hundred thousand or more refugees that are scattered outside their own land. It is with the continuity of the Tibetan spirit that this book is concerned.

Our story is many-layered, and although this book is divided into four parts, there must be a good deal of overlap in every way. The four sections are by no means exclusive: this first one deals with the origins of Tibetan culture and religion, and the second deals with the 'old' Tibet. But the 'old' Tibet was beginning to disappear during the reign, and under the guidance, of the Great Thirteenth Dalai Lama, and a Tibet of the future was already emerging; conversely, many facets of the 'old' Tibet continued even after the Chinese invasion in 1949, though after 1959 Chinese attempts to destroy Tibetan culture were redoubled. The third section of the book deals with occupied Tibet, and with the struggles of the Tibetan people against the Chinese invaders. Although 1959 is the year now commemorated as the time of the National Uprising, there had been a resistance movement against Chinese occupation from the very beginning, and ever-increasing Chinese oppression brought this into the open as early as 1952, when the *Mimang Tsogdu* or 'People's Movement' was started in Lhasa, and parts of Kham first rose in arms in June 1956. As for the fourth part, which deals with exiles, the exiles do not stand alone. There is still a constant trickle of refugees leaving Tibet, and the 'liberalisations' of the early 1980s saw an increased traffic in visitors in both directions, though any Tibetan leaving Tibet normally has to leave a family member as a hostage with the Chinese authorities, in order to ensure their return and to make certain that they behave 'properly' while outside Tibet.

Furthermore, despite the most determined efforts of the Chinese, Tibetan culture is not utterly destroyed in Tibet. The clothes may be old and worn and dirty and ragged – but they are Tibetan clothes, not Chinese. The monasteries may have been shelled and bombed and used as stables, and the paintings of the Buddha may have had the eyes scratched out; the solid gold statues, encrusted with gems, which ornamented the temples, may have been looted and sold to the West; but in each and every home, there is an altar. If it is not safe to

Above *The larger monasteries of old Tibet were the size of villages or even small towns, and required a corresponding amount of administration. A gathering of monks like this was not at all unusual; in fact, it is remarkable that it was photographed at all.*

Opposite *Heavy sheepskin* chubas *are particularly characteristic of nomads. Tibetans continue to wear them even under Chinese rule, partly because they are so practical but also because they are Tibetan, not Chinese. These worn and patched clothes contrast sharply with the new* chubas *in Chinese propaganda photographs.*

Right *The great monasteries were all destroyed, in varying degrees, by the Chinese invaders. This picture shows the ruins of Gaden.*

show the altar in public, the images may be concealed; if a concealed altar has been found and confiscated or destroyed, the shrine is kept within the heart.

There is also a great continuity between Tibetan culture within the geographical boundaries of Tibet and Tibetan culture in exile. Moreover, many border areas such as Ladakh, Zanskar, Lahaul and Spiti, Kinnaur, Sikkim, and Arunachal Pradesh have a culture which is predominantly Tibetan, and in the Tibetan refugee settlements in India the traditions continue. Many of the monasteries of Tibet have been re-established in India; for example, the three great Lhasa monasteries of Ganden, Sera, and Drepung were re-established in Karnataka State in southern India. Sera is in Bylakuppe, about fifty miles from Mysore City, and Ganden and Drepung are less than a hundred miles away in Mundgod. Young monks still join the monasteries at the age of five or six (though they are discouraged from joining until they are older), and they learn to write in the same way that their teachers did in Tibet: with a bamboo pen, on a board lightly coated with chalk dust.

To anyone unfamiliar with Buddhism as practised in Tibet, the whole Tibetan lifestyle may seem strange or even bizarre. For this reason, it is worth looking at Tibetan Buddhism before going on to the three main sections of the book. It is also worth taking a look at the history of Tibet, in order to set the scene for what follows. This is not the place for a scholarly study of Tibetan Buddhism, still less a complete history: there are plenty of books for the religious devotee or the academic. Rather, it is an attempt to capture the mood or flavour of Tibet and the Tibetan people, and to sketch a mood or feeling which captivates almost everyone who comes into contact with it.

About five hundred years before the birth of Christ – according to the strongest traditions, in 544 BC – a son was born to Queen Maya of the princely house of Shakya. She was returning to her parents' home to have her first child, as was the custom, but the child was born before she reached them, so he was born in Lumbini in what is now Nepal. Astrologers predicted that the child would be either a great religious leader, or a great secular prince. His father preferred the latter: the Queen Maya had been his bride for twenty years, and this was their first son, whom he called Siddhartha, which means 'Every Wish Fulfilled'. He ordered that his son be brought up surrounded with the utmost luxury, shielded from any intimation of suffering which might cause him to leave the palace and his parents in order to lead a religious life.

The prince was already married and the father of a son

The Buddha who founded Buddhism in its present form is by no means the only Buddha. We all have the seeds of our own Buddha-nature, and we live in the Age of a Thousand Buddhas. This is Maitreya, the Buddha of the Age to Come.

As well as images of the Buddha, the various Boddhisattvas, and so forth, mantras *were carved on rocks all over Tibet. They furnish a constant reminder of the teachings of the Buddha.*

The Dorje *(thunderbolt) and* Drilbu *(bell) are fundamental symbols of Tibetan Buddhism; it is no exaggeration to call them spiritual tools.*

when he first came into contact with disease, the suffering of old age, and death. It troubled him greatly to know that life was not as he had been led to believe, but was full of suffering. Shortly after this experience, though, he met a wandering mystic who showed him that the suffering of the world might be overcome by right practice. Realising that his upbringing had been grossly distorted, he left his wife and child and became a wandering mystic himself.

Reacting against the luxury of his life up to that point, he went to the other extreme. He spurned all comfort, neglected his body, and mortified his flesh. At last, weakened by years of privation, he fainted from hunger and exhaustion. When he came to, he recognised that this path was as fruitless and distorted as the path of luxury which he had known before. Realising this, he set forth upon what has become known as the Middle Path – the path in which the body is well treated, as befits the house of the soul, but not pampered in a way which would distract it from spiritual activity.

At Bodh Gayā he sat under a Bo or Bodhi tree, determined to meditate upon the Path which he should follow. He already knew that it was a path of moderation, but according to tradition he made a surprisingly immoderate vow:

Blood may become exhausted, flesh may decay, bones may fall apart, but I shall never leave this place until I find the way to Enlightenment.

At the age of thirty-five, he arrived at an understanding which was so profound that thereafter he was known as the Buddha, or Enlightened One. What he formulated as a result of his insight is known as the Four Noble Truths, as follows:

(1) Existence is inherently unsatisfactory and full of suffering; otherwise, why should anyone be unhappy?

(2) Unsatisfactoriness or suffering is caused by desire. Desire is what makes us want what we do not have, which is what makes us unhappy.

(3) If we can rid ourselves of desire, we can rid ourselves of unhappiness.

(4) We can rid ourselves of desire by training the mind, which is done by following a path based on:
Right Understanding (of the nature of things)
Right Purpose (in undertaking anything)
Right Speech
Right Conduct (towards others)
Right Vocation (that harms no one)
Right Effort
Right Alertness (in knowing when to act)
Right Concentration (or not being distracted).

These eight 'Rights' are known as the Eightfold Path, which is often represented as a wheel with eight spokes.

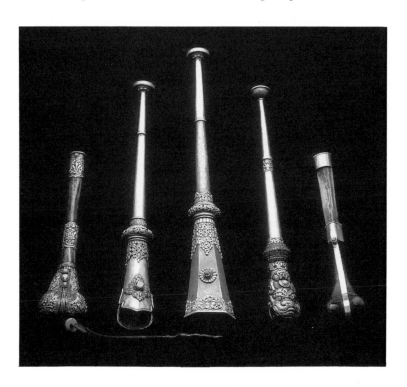

Kanglings used by ngakpas *are traditionally made from human thigh bones, like the outer two in this picture, but those for monastic use are usually made of copper, silver, and gold.*

The names by which the Four Noble Truths are known vary, but a common set of names is:

For the First Noble Truth: the Noble Truth of Suffering

For the Second Noble Truth: the Noble Truth of the Cause of Suffering

For the Third Noble Truth: the Noble Truth of the Cessation of the Cause of Suffering

For the Fourth Noble Truth: the Noble Truth of the Means of the Cessation of the Cause of Suffering.

Whatever they are called, it is hard to argue against them. It is also clear that there is no sign of a God, which immediately raises two questions. The first is how you can have a religion without a God, and the second is why there appear to be so many 'gods' and 'goddesses' in Tibetan Buddhism.

The first question is not really answerable; it is merely a question of how you choose to define a religion. It does explain, however, why Buddhism is referred to by some as a 'science of the mind', rather than as a religion. Alternatively, there is something that His Holiness the Fourteenth Dalai Lama says, which is that the basis of all religion is a willingness to help others and to try to make the world a better place. As he explains it, religion is an expression of what he calls 'universal responsibility and the good heart', rather than its cause. By this definition, Buddhism is as much a religion as any other, and because it is based on logic and understanding, rather than on blind faith, it cannot as readily be used as some religions by bigots or advocates of sectarianism and intolerance. The Buddha himself told his followers to test every word as a goldsmith tests gold: rub it, scrape it, melt it, and only accept it as good if it stands up to all the tests.

The second question is more difficult to answer. The Buddha's teaching stressed the way in which each and every individual is responsible for achieving enlightenment for himself or herself. This is the basis of the oldest school of Buddhism, which is known as the Therevada (the Way of the Elders) or the Hinayana (the Lesser Vehicle). A later school, which arose about five hundred years after the Buddha's death, pointed out that he had not selfishly kept his secret to himself: rather, he had shared it with the world out of his compassion for all sentient beings. This broader emphasis on working for the good of all beings rather than just for oneself led to the new school being called the Mahayana, or Greater Vehicle, and it is in this school that we come across the profusion of 'gods' and 'goddesses'.

In fact, these terms are very confusing to many Westerners.

Representations of the Buddha are common throughout the Buddhist world, but in Tibet they are joined by representations of many other Lha *and* Lhamo *figures.*

On the one hand 'gods' and 'goddesses' are inhabitants of a higher level of existence than human beings, though not 'divine' in any Judaeo-Christian sense: they are called *Lha* and *Lhamo* (-*mo* is the feminine suffix), and represent one of the six realms of existence. Because they are still in a realm of duality, though, their position is in many ways similar to that of human beings: they can be reborn as humans, just as humans have the potential to be reborn in *Lha.yul*, and it is possible for humans to reach higher levels of spiritual attainment. On the other hand, many of what the Westerners call 'gods' are actually Bodhisattvas, those who have attained enlightenment and thus freedom from the necessity to return to the cyclic realm of existence, but who choose to remain within this realm in order to help all sentient beings: Chenrezig (Avalokiteśvara), Dorje-Sempa (Vajrasattva), and Dolma (Tara) are all examples of Bodhisattvas who attained enlightenment aeons in the past, but who assumed the Bodhisattva role in order to help sentient beings – that is, beings in the six realms. Furthermore, by meditating upon the nature of these Bodhisattvas, and their vows, the Buddhist can begin to understand how the Bodhisattva's path might be followed.

To the Hinayana and the Mahayana is added the Vajrayana, or Thunderbolt Path (though 'Vajra' is also correctly translated as 'Diamond' or 'Adamantine'). This is often viewed as a third school, but a more orthodox view would be that it is one of the two divisions of the Mahayana, the other being the Sutrayana. It is a short, fast path as its name implies, but for

Though this ngakpa *is very obviously posing for a picture, the topknot, the white* Tumo *skirt, the* chod *drum, and the trumpet* (Kangling) *made from a human thigh-bone are all characteristic.*

that reason it is more demanding than the other vehicles. Its flavour is distinctly magical, though to equate it with Western black magic is quite meaningless: rather, it is concerned with self-knowledge in a very fundamental and often dramatic way. For example, the celebrated *Chöd* practice (the word means 'cutting', as in 'cutting attachment') is performed in a graveyard: the practitioner visualises ghouls and demons which eat his body. Insufficient skill can result in one of two things: failure, and a waste of time, or madness, if the practitioner fails to control his own mind. Such practices should not be lightly undertaken, but if they are successful, the practitioner has gone a long way towards ridding himself of the 'three poisons' or 'three affective emotions' of attraction, aversion, and indifference (or ignorance). On closer examination, these three poisons turn out to be the three different ways in which desire (as in the Second Noble Truth) can manifest itself.

Viewed in the light of the Vajrayana, the myriad deities and demons make much more sense, with each symbolising a particular aspect of Buddha-nature which we wish to obtain. Although this is a fascinating subject, and one on which countless books have been written, this is not the place to write more. Plenty of other books are available, and perhaps the best way to approach them is in accordance with the Dalai Lama's advice:

> Outwardly, practice Hinayana
> Inwardly, practice Mahayana
> Secretly, practice Vajrayana.

These different schools, which arose in India, were influenced in Tibet by the native Bon religion – which still exists, and in which it is possible to find similarities with Buddhism. To an outsider, the similarities are perhaps more striking than they are to a practitioner of either religion, as Bon has a mystical flavour similar to the oldest (Nyingma) order of Buddhism in Tibet. The result of the intermingling of a thousand years of Buddhist tradition with a thousand years of Bonpo tradition in the latter part of the first millennium AD was that religion probably played a greater part in life in Tibet than in any other country in the world at any time, whether it was the religion of the lay people, the religion of the monks (whose lives would not have been very different from their Christian contemporaries), or the religion of the *ngakpas* or Tantric practitioners (Tantrayana = Vajrayana).

Of course, none of this answers the question of *why* Tibet should be such a religious state. A modern answer, given almost as a reflex, might be that the country was priest-ridden, and that everyone followed religion in fear; but this was and is utterly untrue. Certainly, the monasteries had considerable economic power, both by wealth and by weight of numbers, but lamas were not feared, and only a very few lived in anything which might be called even a semblance of luxury. A more accurate answer might be that Tibetans are naturally friendly and considerate, and that the teaching of the Buddha accorded so well with their natural inclinations that it was not a question of their living 'under' Buddhism: Buddhism simply meshed with their world-picture. Even this only goes a very small way towards explaining the fusion of state and religion, though; another answer may be sought in the history of the country.

The Tibetan Royal Year (*Bod-rGyal-Lo*) calendar is reckoned from the year when Nyatri Tsenpo was proclaimed the first King of Tibet – 127 BC in the Christian reckoning. For centuries after the foundation of the nation, Tibet was a warlike country, and by the ninth century of the Tibetan era, or the eighth century of the Christian calendar, it had acquired a huge empire that stretched well down into India to the south and to China in the east. So powerful was Tibet that in AD 763, during the reign of Trisong Detsen, the Tibetan army not only captured Ho-Shi and Lungyu, the two westernmost provinces of China, but even marched into the then capital of China, Ch'ang-an, and established the prince of Kuang-wu as their own puppet emperor under the title of Tashi – though admittedly he was deposed after the Tibetan army withdrew. The victory is recorded on the famous stone pillar which still stands in Lhasa to this day, the Zhol Doring. The text is damaged, by time and by people banging stones against the pillar either to gain souvenirs or (according to some sources) for good luck, but much of it can still be read. The dotted lines later in the inscription represent areas where the text is illegible; it reads (in part):

The Zhol Doring, *the long stone which records the treaty between the victorious Tibetans and the conquered Chinese in the late 8th century.*

> ...King Trisong Detsen, being a profound man, the breadth of his counsel was extensive, and whatever he did for the kingdom was completely successful. He conquered and held under his sway many districts and fortresses of China. The Chinese Emperor, Hehu Ki Wang, and his Ministers were terrified. They offered a perpetual yearly tribute of 50,000 rolls of silk, and China was obliged to pay this tribute. When the Chinese Emperor, Hehu Ki Wang the father, died, the son Wang Peng Wang succeeded to the throne. He was not able to pay tribute to Tibet, and the King of

Tibet was offended. Nganlam Lukhong took the lead in counsels for the launching of war against China's centre, at the Chinese Emperor's palace Keng-shir. Shangchim Gyalzig Shultheng and Takdra Lukhong were appointed as the two chief commanders for the campaign against Keng-shir. They attacked Keng-shir and a great battle was fought with the Chinese on the banks of the Chow-chi. The Chinese were put to flight and many were killed.

The Chinese Emperor, Wang Pen Wang, left the fort in Keng-shir and fled to Shem-chow. The Ministers of the Interior, Chewu Keng, Don Kyan, and So Kyan... subjects of (Tibetan) King...Tibet... Kow-wang, the younger brother of Kim-shing Kung-chu, was made Emperor of China... minister...vassals, great and small...the (Tibetan) Empire was firmly established and its fame and praise were spread abroad. Lukhong being in the King's confidence took great trouble for the good of the kingdom.

It was in the middle of the seventh century AD, however, that the great Tibetan King Songtsen Gampo had obliged the Emperor of China to send him a daughter as a diplomatic bride. Both the Chinese princess and a Nepalese diplomatic bride were Buddhists, and despite the fact that the King also had Bonpo brides, he became converted to their religion, thereby establishing a seed which was to bloom in unimaginable glory in Tibet. A hundred years later, in AD 747, a great Indian teacher called Padmasambhava or 'The Lotus Born' was invited to the Roof of the World. Endowed with tremendous mystical powers, as well as skilled in debate and in the study of the Dharma (the body of Buddhist teaching), he travelled widely, subduing demons and performing miracles: so great was his influence that he became known as Guru Rinpoche, the Precious Teacher, among his other names. The oldest order of Buddhists in Tibet, the Nyingmapa (the word means Ancient Order) traces its teaching lineages back to Guru Rinpoche.

Under King Trisong Detsen, who reigned AD 755-97, Buddhism also became the official court religion, though at first it did not have the dramatic pacifist influence which it was to have later: even in the reign of Ngadak Triral (AD 815-36), Tibet was still conducting wars of conquest. But slowly, in the words of the Tibetan phrase, the Tibetan people 'laid their weapons at the feet of the Lotus Throne' – the throne, that is, of the Buddha.

There was a brief interlude in the ninth century AD when

Guru Rinpoche introduced Buddhism to Tibet, and the oldest surviving order of Tibetan Buddhism traces its teaching lineages back to him. Rupas or statues of lineage teachers add to the tremendous visual richness of a Tibetan shrine.

King Lang Darma tried to suppress Buddhism and restore the warlike nature of his country, but he was assassinated in AD 842 (by a Buddhist monk!) and the progress of Buddhism continued. After the Nyingmapa came the Kagyudpa, the Sakyapa, and finally the Gelugpa, to give the four orders of Tibetan Buddhism which survive today; in the Tibetan constitution, these four orders and the Bonpo each have a seat, as of right, in the Government.

An almost inevitable consequence of this spiritualisation of the country was, however, the collapse of central secular organisation and a power struggle between petty princelings and prelates. Curiously, the Golden Horde never seriously attacked Tibet, and the Tibetan view of Mongol history is surprisingly different from the commonly accepted version – surprising, that is, until you realise the source of the commonly accepted version, which is of course Persian and Chinese. Both of these great empires present the Mongols as cruel and tyrannical, but both were soundly trounced by the Mongols and neither has ever been at a loss when it came to devising tortures and atrocities of their own; their 'historical' view of the Mongols is, therefore, tainted both by self-justification and by propaganda. The Tibetans, on the other hand, have no particular axe to grind, and their histories show the Khans as open-minded and tolerant – and prepared to oppose intolerance to the death.

The days of Tibetan military greatness, now a thousand years in the past, are commemorated by antique arms and armour which were kept purely for ceremonial purposes.

Although Tibetan Buddhists are pacifists, they have always been ready to defend themselves. The odd-looking prongs on the rifles (mostly Lee Enfield and Lee Metford .303 British army models) are antelope horns used to steady the gun, after the fashion of a Bren-gun bipod. Note the ferocious swords: weapons like these were successfully used against Chinese machine-gunners. Their success was not due to any lack of bravery on the part of the Chinese, but to the bravery born of desperation of the Tibetans. This picture was shot by Heinrich Harrer in the 1940s or 1950s, but similar bands fought the Chinese into the 1960s.

The connection between the two nations began well before the establishment of the Yüan dynasty. In AD 1244 Godan Khan, Genghis Khan's grandson, issued an invitation to Sakyapandita Kunga Gyaltsen. In AD 1247 the two men met in the Kokonor region, and thereafter Sakyapandita Kunga Gyaltsen instructed the Mongol Khan in the teachings of the Buddha, as well as acting as a kind of ambassador for Tibet. Before he died, Kunga Gyaltsen passed his spiritual authority to his nephew, Sakya Lodoe Gyaltsen (more often known as Sakya Phagpa), who was in turn invited to the court of Kublai Khan in AD 1253, and who so impressed the Mongol that he was asked to give religious instruction to the Khan and his Ministers. According to tradition, Sakya Phagpa bestowed consecration on twenty-five of Kublai Khan's ministers, on three separate occasions. On the first occasion, he received in return spiritual and temporal authority over the thirteen myriarchies (Trikor Chuksum) of Central Tibet; on the second, a relic of the Buddha and authority over U-Tsang, Kham (Do-Tod) and Amdo (Do-med), collectively known as

Chol-kha-sum; and on the third, the title of Tishri or 'Imperial Preceptor'.

At this time, Kublai Khan had not yet founded the Yüan dynasty in China – this was not to happen until 1279 or (according to some sources) 1280 – but he was in command of the Kokonor region, and his star was very much in the ascendant. It is in large part upon his supposed grants of power to Sakya Phagpa that Chinese claims to 'suzerainty' over Tibet rest; certainly, Mongol might established Sakya rule in Tibet.

In 1358, however, Situ Changchub Gyaltsen managed to wrest political power from the Sakya minister Wangtson, and the temporal link with the Mongols was severed, although there was still considerable religious intercourse. The Mongol Yüan dynasty ended in China ten years later, in 1368.

In 1578 the temporal connection was renewed when Sonam Gyatso, the third in a line of great Gelugpa teachers, finally met Altan Khan, one of the most important Mongol rulers, at the Mongol's request. Altan Khan sent a large delegation with camels, horses, and provisions to escort the Tibetan, and came to meet him: the two men journeyed together to the chief town of the Mongols, a place whose location is now uncertain,

Tibetan militias were often organised on a local basis; this picture, probably taken in the 1920s, shows the motley collection of long guns and the leader with a Mauser pistol.

but which was known to the Tibetans as Khar Ngonpo (the Blue Fort), or as Koko Kotan (the Blue Town). There they swore friendship and exchanged titles. The Tibetan called the Mongolian 'Majestic Purity, King of Religion', and the Mongolian called Sonam Gyatso 'Great Ocean Teacher', meaning, 'The Teacher Whose Wisdom is as Vast as the Ocean'. In the Mongolian tongue, this is 'Dalai Lama'.

The principle of reincarnating teachers was accepted in all schools of Tibetan Buddhism by this time, and because Sonam Gyatso was the third in his line, the title was retrospectively applied to the two previous incarnations, and he was known as the Third Dalai Lama. Unlike ordinary people, who go to the Bardo state and take rebirth because they have no choice, the great reincarnating teachers 'retire to the honourable fields' between incarnations, and choose when and to what parents they are reborn. The departing incarnation usually leaves signs concerning where he will be reborn, and after his death search parties are sent out to find the new incarnation. When they find the child whom they suspect may be the reincarnation, one of the tests is to ask him to choose between pairs of similar objects, one of which he had owned in his past life, and one of which is a decoy. A full account of the discovery of the present Dalai Lama is to be found in His Holiness's own autobiography *My Land and My People* (which goes up to the age of 25 or so), or in *Great Ocean*, an authorised biography of the Dalai Lama written by Ngakpa Chögyam and myself.

To the Dalai Lama's religious influence (which was already considerable) there was now added powerful temporal influence: the Mongol Khan and the Tibetan Lama agreed that henceforth there should flourish, as of old, a unique 'Priest-Patron' relationship, in which the Mongols would protect the Tibetans and guard their spiritual welfare in return for the Tibetans teaching the Mongols about Buddhism and acting as their spiritual mentors. The Fourth Dalai Lama was actually a Mongolian by birth, the only non-Tibetan Dalai Lama to date.

It was the Fifth Dalai Lama, however, who put the seal on the position of the Dalai Lama as the head of both the religion and the state in Tibet. With the support of Gushri Khan, he was formally installed in AD 1642 as the King of Tibet, a position which the Dalai Lama has held ever since. The Fifth Dalai Lama is generally known as the Great Fifth for many reasons: his religious merit, the work he did in uniting Tibet, and his structuring of the Tibetan government, with one monk and one lay official in most key posts, so that both the secular and the religious should have a hand in determining policy.

There was also an organised Tibetan army, and after investigating various European armies, the Great Thirteenth Dalai Lama modelled his army on the British one. Chamba Tendhar who appears in this photograph was the Commander in Chief in Kham.

This was, however, to be the high point of the Dalai Lama's power for almost two and a half centuries. Gushri Khan died in 1655, and in him died the last of the great Mongol war-lords: Mongol armies could no longer guarantee Tibet's security. The newly reunited Tibetan nation was still fragile, and when the Great Fifth died in 1682, his Prime Minister (*Desi*) concealed news of his death in order to allow the completion of the great Potala Palace which had already been started, and which would serve as a powerful symbol of a united Tibet. There may also have been many other reasons; the Desi could no doubt foresee the danger of a Chinese invasion by the increasingly strong Manchu dynasty, and of possible civil unrest, which had bordered on civil war even in the days when the Great Fifth had first come to power. He must also have feared that a Regent would be appointed who might detract from his own position, because he had been the favourite of the Great Fifth and had enjoyed his utmost confidence. Accordingly, he found a monk who could pass

The devoutness of Tibetan Buddhists is legendary, and has not been diminished either by the Chinese or by exile. As an aside, this old lady's ear-ring is supported in the traditional Tibetan fashion with a loop of string, as well as passing through the pierced ear.

Opposite *Tibet is not an easy country to invade, as these buildings perched precariously on a rock-face show. It was not until late in the twentieth century that air transport and telecommunications made it possible to establish more than a loose, consensus rule over the whole country.*

for the Great Fifth at a distance for state occasions, and the general public were told that His Holiness had entered upon a retreat which might last for several years.

The search was nevertheless instigated for the Sixth Dalai Lama, who was found and brought up in secret. The Potala was completed in 1695, and in 1696 the Desi revealed that the Great Fifth had died fourteen years earlier; the Sixth was enthroned in 1697, but turned out to be a considerable embarrassment to the Regent. He refused to take his final monastic vows, and he was a self-avowed lover of wine and women:

> Oh, with my true dear love
> If I could but be wed
> To win gems from the Ocean's depth
> Cannot compare with this joy

or

> To the learned Lama
> I went to learn the Dharma
> Unchanged, my stony heart
> Has flown to my sweetheart!

or again

> As if to love my heart
> To the Dharma inclined
> In this single lifetime
> I could Nirvana attain
>   (Trans. Lhasang Tsering)

The great Peak Potala in Lhasa is probably the best known symbol of Tibet in the outside world. It was built during the second half of the seventeenth century C.E., during and after the reign of the Great Fifth Dalai Lama.

Many people do not appreciate that there are great lakes and rivers in Tibet, which make travelling difficult. The river valleys are often well-sheltered and very fertile.

Opposite *Yaks, sheep, and goats were the main source of wealth in old Tibet, and the life-style was mainly pastoral.*

Above *The Circumambulation of holy buildings has always been a characteristic of Tibetan religion; here you can see the whirling prayer wheels (sridpa khorlo) in the right hand and the rosary (tengwar) in the left. The shadow of Peter Aufschnaiter with his Leica is in the extreme left-hand corner.*

Right *Prayer wheels are filled with mantras – a word which translates as something between 'prayers' and 'spells' – and are spun as a reminder of the teachings of Buddhism. They are not a 'mechanised' form of prayer, but an aid to right-mindfulness: spinning a prayer wheel without awareness is about as meaningful as spinning the handle on a coffee grinder.*

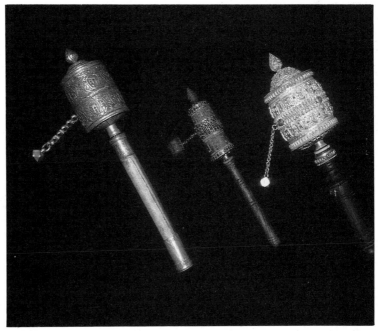

Even so, the Tibetan people refused to hear any ill of him. He had not taken vows of celibacy, and a life such as his was not incompatible with the Vajrayana. Moreover, they argued, even as he was out carousing in Lhasa, he was simultaneously meditating in another body-manifestation in the Potala, the great fortress-palace which dominates Lhasa and which was begun in the reign of the Great Fifth. It is also believed that his sexual activity was of Tantric foundation; as he wrote

> Never have I slept without a sweetheart
> Nor have I spent a single drop of sperm
> (Trans. K Dhondup)

Whatever he did, he did not take part in the government of Tibet in the same way as his predecessor, and according

The fondness of Lhasa people for parties is a byword in Tibet, and this elaborate outdoor affair is by no means unusual.

to the official histories he was supposed to have died at the hands of the Manchus in 1706 – though another tradition, written in the *Secret Biography of the Sixth Dalai Lama*, says that he escaped death and went on to teach in many places in Tibet, Mongolia, Nepal, possibly India, and even China, before dying in Mongolia in 1746. Even then, his gift for bi-location was such that he is said to have two tombs, and the Seventh was discovered long before 1746.

The Seventh and Eighth Dalai Lamas were more concerned with the spiritual realm than with the temporal, although in the case of the Seventh this was to a large extent the doing of the Regent, who tried to keep the temporal power for himself; the Eighth did not enjoy good health, and although he was requested to take temporal rule, he preferred to keep a prime minister to handle temporal affairs. The Ninth, Tenth, Eleventh and Twelfth all died very young, probably as a result of Manchu-inspired assassinations by poison; the Manchus assiduously courted the Regents, and by the middle of the nineteenth century the Manchu influence was at its peak in Tibet – which is another foundation for modern Chinese claims to 'suzerainty' over Tibet.

The Great Thirteenth Dalai Lama, born in 1876, completely reversed this creeping foreign influence. From the very start, he showed himself to be in the tradition of the Great Fifth, an able administrator as well as a great lama. When the British invaded Tibet in 1904 in order to extract a trade treaty he fled to Mongolia, traditionally a second home for the Dalai Lama. His return was deliberately delayed by the Manchus, who took advantage of his absence to launch a Chinese invasion which began in 1905. He returned to Lhasa in 1909 but was forced to flee once again in 1910, only a few months later with an invading army at his gates. This time he fled to British India, as we shall see in the next chapter.

Although the British declined to intervene on the Tibetans' behalf, they did treat the Dalai Lama very well, and with the collapse of the Manchu dynasty in 1911/12, the Tibetans were able to evict the Manchu Ambans and their troops without any external help. In 1913 the Great Thirteenth returned to Lhasa and formally reaffirmed Tibetan independence. The next two decades of his reign were to prove singularly enlightened: he introduced to Tibet many of the trappings of a modern independent state, including its own currency; its own postal and telegraph systems; Western-style schools (he also sent four Tibetan boys to Rugby school in England); and a reformed and modernised army. Unfortunately, this 'revolution from the top' was countered at every stage by the monasteries, who did their very best to ensure that the old order changed as little as possible.

This is the point at which criticisms of Tibet as being reactionary and priest-ridden become fair. The Great Thirteenth Dalai Lama himself, in what is now known as his Political Testament, prophesied what would happen if Tibet did not modernise: the country would be invaded by a power which would try to wipe both Tibetan culture and the teachings of the Buddha from the face of the earth. On the other hand, there was an embryonic but growing foreign trade, and the cruel punishments which had been common when Manchu influence was at its height were abolished, except in the case

The Great Thirteenth Dalai Lama, who would have been the founder of a modern Tibet if only he had had the chance.

of a very few crimes such as stealing from temples and murdering high lamas. It would be fair to compare the standards of the Tibet of that period with those of mediaeval Europe; and Tibet would compare very favourably. But even by the standards of the late twentieth century, Tibet was by no means a bad place to live. It may have lacked the material wealth of the West, but its spiritual development was unparalleled, justice was commonplace and the right of all (the Great Thirteenth instituted a sort of reverse secret police, to seek out and eradicate abuses of power by officials), and there was no religious intolerance: Buddhists, Bonpo, Hindus, Moslems, and Christians lived in amity. It was, in fact, a country which embodied a genuine attempt to put into practice the teachings of the Buddha.

OLD TIBET

In the West today, 'feudal' is a term of abuse. On its own, it conjures up images of idle and oppressive landlords living off downtrodden peasants; and when 'religion' is considered as well, all sorts of popular stereotypes come to mind. This is why the usual description of Tibet as 'feudal' is as much misleading as it is informative.

To begin with, Tibetan feudalism was never the same as Western feudalism, which was always militarily based. Secondly, feudal societies can have their advantages: justly administered, they can provide the same 'safety net' of security which we associate with a modern welfare state, even if they cannot provide the same standard of living. Thirdly, mobility has always been possible in Tibetan society, especially through the paths of monastic administration but also through the paths of secular administration. And finally, Tibetan feudalism changed considerably in the first half of the twentieth century. Western influences came in via the British Raj in India; there was a small but steadily growing merchant class, and all kinds of international goods were being imported in increasing quantities; and as we have seen, the Dalai Lama himself was actively trying to reform and modernise his country.

There was never an official census of Tibet, but a good estimate based on figures from the monasteries and *dzongs* (administrative centres) indicates a population of about six million, mostly concentrated in the fertile east of the country, in Kham and Amdo. These Tibetan provinces are now claimed by the Chinese as part of China, which explains why the Chinese always quote the population of Tibet as under two million.

Tibet is a country of surprising diversity. It is ringed by mountains on the northern, western, and southern borders, but only the north-west of the country is almost completely inhospitable, a wasteland of titanic mountains, vast empty landscapes strewn with shattered rocks, and utter desolation. It is beautiful, but it is a beauty with no shelter: it affords little

opportunity for settling and making a living. Similar scenes are to be found in many areas of Tibet, but they are softened by the proximity of sheltered valleys in which many crops are grown – the staple barley, peas, and even apricots. These valleys are the home of agriculture in Tibet, for although the growing season is short, self-sufficiency is possible and indeed essential. The less sheltered areas are high pampas, grass country where the variety of grasses is remarkable: in some places, the tallest plant as far as the eye can see may be no more than six inches high, while in other parts the grass grows higher than a man's head. At night, in the high, clear air of Tibet, the colours of the individual stars can be seen.

This picture captures the popular image of Tibet, but in reality it is only the west and (particularly) the north-west which is so unrelievedly bleak. Elsewhere, there are sheltered and fertile valleys.

The first Tibetans were probably nomads, hunters at first and then farmers, following the great herds of yak as they in turn followed the seasonal grazing, and living in tents of yak-wool, but in many areas they settled down to a combination of agriculture and herding: land and cattle were the basis of secular wealth in Tibet, though sheep and goats (bred for milk and wool, as well as meat) were also very important. The yak provided not only meat, milk, butter, and dung for fires, but also leather, sinew, bone for carving, and wool: the coarse outer hair could be woven only with difficulty, but the soft inner coat can yield very delicate fabrics. (Incidentally, although 'yak' is used in the West as the generic term for Tibetan cattle, '*yak*' is the masculine and '*dri*' the femine ('bull' and 'cow'), so to talk of 'yak's milk' and 'yak butter' is a mistake to amuse anyone who realises the difference!) Both sheep and yak wool were spun, dyed, and woven at home: once again, self-sufficiency was the watchword. One other interesting point about sheep and goats is that they were used as beasts of burden: yaks were of course one of the main draught and transport animals, but pack-mules, pack-sheep, and pack-goats were also usual.

Much of Tibet is high desert, with scrubby vegetation. Building on rocky outcrops gives a commanding view of the surrounding countryside and makes for easy defence against anything but heavy artillery and air attack, but there is also a mystical or devotional reason for building monasteries on high and inaccessible places: many parallels can be found in Europe, especially on Mount Athos in Greece.

The hardy yak (female dri*) and its cross with domestic cattle, the* dzo*, are the animals which everyone associates with Tibet.*

Opposite above *Domesticated yaks, often used as beasts of burden, are usually smaller and less powerfully built than wild ones.*

Opposite below *Even boat builders rely on the yak; coracles such as these are made of yak-hide.*

Right *The wool of yaks, sheep and goats were all woven in Tibet, but one of the finest fabrics was woven from the soft under-hair of the yak; a strip of cloth of this type could be pulled through a wedding ring, it was so light and soft.*

Below *Carpet-weaving, one of the staple sources of income of Tibetans in exile, was also widespread in Tibet. The carpet looms were collapsible (though the beams were fairly substantial) and a carpet-weaver might well set up her loom in the house of a wealthy patron so that she could weave a carpet to order.*

There are few nomads left now. Because of their mobile lifestyle, and the difficulty of access to their traditional grazing grounds, it took longer for the Chinese to communise them and to subject them to Maoist thought than it took in the villages, but the ways in which they tried to control these wanderers were truly bizarre. First, they tried to settle them in permanent sites, forcing them to build stone houses and telling them to administer their cattle (which had been confiscated and re-allocated, after the removal of a few animals for provisioning the Chinese army) 'collectively'. They also told them to grow grain – which, predictably, failed. Next, they ordered the nomads to 'cultivate' grass as fodder, by fencing in large areas of grassland. When this, too, failed their solution was to increase the number of yaks by deliberate breeding, regardless of the fact that there was not enough grass or salt to support them in the restricted areas in which the nomads were permitted to move – so the dri did not even provide milk or butter. Eventually, with starvation rampant, the Chinese were forced to allow the nomads to resume something resembling their old lifestyle, though they returned to a land where there were now very few wild yaks left, because Chinese soldiers had slaughtered them with machine-guns, for 'sport' and food.

Although for many years the emphasis in Tibetan culture has been shifting from the nomadic life to farming, and even

to town and city life, the influence of the nomadic lifestyle can be seen in many aspects of Tibetan culture, even in the towns and cities and in exile. One of the most obvious examples is the use of tents and awnings. The Tibetan sun can be fierce, and awnings to protect participants in a religious ceremony on the roof of the temple, or the spectators at a *Lhamo* folk opera performance, are common sense; but even in exile, the Dalai Lama speaks on National Uprising Day from his own yellow throne-tent, and other tents are set up to protect the accompanying dignitaries. At an open day for the parents of young monks at a monastery, tents like small English garden-party marquees will be set up; an enormous awning, the 'Inner Sky', covers the outdoor stage at a Lhamo performance.

Rather less obvious is the way in which everything is made portable. The tall tea-churns can be slung over the shoulder like a rifle; the ubiquitous carpets used as seats and sleeping-mats can be rolled; the cushions which go under them fold in half; and even the tables are made to fold. In religious life, the silk *thangkas* (religious scroll-paintings) can be rolled, the mighty *dung-chen* or eight-foot 'great horn' telescopes down to no more than a yard long, the offering bowls filled with water can be emptied and stacked one inside the other, and the mandala set, which looks like a many-tiered wedding cake when it is filled with barley or rice, collapses to no more than a set of silver rings, each three or four inches high and fitting one inside the next like a set of pastry cutters.

Awnings kept the fierce Tibetan sun off the heads of these noble ladies. The more elaborate head-dresses are from central Tibet, the simpler ones from Kham. Tents and awnings play a major part in Tibetan festivities to this day.

The mandala offering set, shown here filled with rice, collapses to nothing more than a set of rings and the top piece for transport.

Permanent dwellings were usually built of stone: thick walled and dark inside, though sun-dried mud-bricks and a sort of rammed-earth construction using wooden shutters to form the walls *in situ* were also used. The interiors were crowded and blackened with smoke both from the yak dung fires (one of the best dried dung fuels, and surprisingly clean and hot-burning) and from the butter lamps burning on the family altar. The poorest houses would not be unfamiliar to a Scottish crofter of the last century, with the beast-house an extension of the main living quarters, but the better houses (in which most people lived, because building a house was a matter of communal effort) would have a beast-house on the bottom floor and living quarters above.

Whether nomad or settled, life for the poor did not vary much, though the villagers were usually more comfortable. The staple food was *tsampa*, barley roasted whole and then ground to a flour. Mixed with black tea and butter to make a dry dough, it is extremely filling (though rather stodgy) and

Tibetan domestic architecture is often inseparable from the rock on which it is built, and caves may sometimes be incorporated in the dwelling-house.

Thangkas (religious paintings) are mounted on spindles, with fabric surrounds, so that they can be rolled for transport. While they are being painted, though, they are stretched tightly across wooden frames.

37

a good deal more edible than it sounds. The best tsampa is delicious; a meal of tsampa, dried yak meat, and good *chang* (barley beer) with a pinch of tsampa in it, is unexpectedly excellent. The thin, dry Tibetan air allowed finger-thick strips of yak meat to be dried naturally, and anyone who has only tried commercially made beef jerky would have to taste the incredibly tender yet tasty yak meat before they could believe how good it can be. Vegetables were never common in Tibet, though they did become rather more fashionable among the well-off as Western influence spread: a Lhasa joke tells of a nomad who visits the capital and then goes back to his people and tells them how poor the people in the city are, but that at least they will never starve. "They have learned to eat grass," he says, "by giving it different kinds of names. They even call one sort of grass by my daughter's name!" *Sonam-Palzom* is a common girl's name, and it is also Tibetan for coriander, a typical ingredient of Tibetan salads.

Tibetan tea is perhaps one of the better-known items of Tibetan cuisine. It is usually reported with loathing by Western visitors, but this is quite unfair. Properly made, with fresh butter, it is very drinkable, but you have to stop thinking of it as tea in the Western sense and think of it as some kind of soup. Brick tea is broken up and boiled with water, then the tea is strained into a tall cylindrical tea-maker with a loose-fitting plunger, and churned with butter, salt, and perhaps a pinch of soda. If it is made with rancid butter, it

Most outsiders, who seldom realise what a beautiful country it is, would not associate a pastoral scene such as this with Tibet, let alone with the western provinces, but it is by no means unusual.

can no doubt be very unpleasant indeed; but subsistence farming means that you cannot afford to throw away butter merely because it goes rancid, and besides, the strong, creamy flavour of butter from the dri or female yak may not always be to the taste of a Westerner.

Butter is a great symbol of hospitality, and even chang is served with a pinch of butter on the side of the bowl. A good hostess will offer dried meat with the chang, and this is one of those occasions when Tibetan hospitality can become somewhat unnerving in the face of Tibetan hygiene. An unwashed thumb scoops out a little butter and puts it on the side of the bowl; the thumb is then wiped casually on the dress, and used to sort through the dried meat, so that only the best pieces are offered to the guest. In the cold dry climate of Tibet, this was less of a problem than it is in India.

The normal form of trade was barter, but in such a bare economy it sufficed: there was no great need of money, though it was minted in both silver and copper, and paper

Although vegetables were not widely eaten, some root vegetables were cultivated both as food for humans and as cattle fodder.

money was printed as well. Often, it was less a matter of barter than of mutual help. When your neighbour built a house, you helped him, because sooner or later you would need his help. Very little was exported from old Tibet, mostly just yak tails, wool, and rock salt, but very little was imported either. Usually, any surplus barley was stored in the granaries of the local *dzong* or monastery granaries, so that if the crops failed there was an insurance against starvation: in Tibet's dry climate, grain could literally be stored for decades. Often, the monks would sell the grain, and apply the funds to the monastery, but they would always make a present of a few *khels* (a measure of about 13 kg) rather than see someone starve. As a result, famine was virtually unknown – until the Chinese came.

Surpluses other than barley were normally sold and traded, and the bulk of the proceeds would normally go towards religion. Some would be in the form of direct donations to monasteries, some would be presented to monks in return for performing religious ceremonies, and some would be spent on the family altar: butter for the lamps, incense, a mandala offering of barley or rice, and *katags* (pronounced 'katas') or ceremonial scarves. A katag is a piece of white cloth about 12 to 18 inches wide and 3 to 6 feet long; originally, it was a piece of cloth brought as a useful gift, but it became ritualised, and katags are now draped over religious statues, presented to lamas as a mark of respect, or exchanged between friends at meetings and partings.

In a village, or among nomads, there would normally be a single headman, and a few other men of rather higher standing than average. The headman's position was normally hereditary, deriving originally from qualities of leadership, but sustained by wealth in the form of cattle and sheep. It was often a semi-elected post, 'semi' in the sense that power would only be taken from the headman (or his son, or the dynasty) if it was misused. In other words, the leaders of a Tibetan village or nomadic band would be 'first among equals', rather than enjoying any special privileges. They might live in a slightly bigger house, and they would probably employ servants and other staff, but their life would not be very different from that of other people. It was regarded in old Tibet as being perfectly proper for anyone, from the lowest farm-hand to the highest aristocracy, to be involved in trade, so an astute businessman could do very well for himself if he could spare the time away from his crops and his animals.

The position of women in Tibet was better than in almost any other oriental country (or in mediaeval Europe, for that

A Dzong. *Although the word means primarily 'fortress' it is also the name given to local administrative centres.*

Katags, *'robes of the gods', are not just exchanged between people; they are also thrown over statues, such as this 20-foot-high statue of Guru Rinpoche carved in the living rock of a cave in which he once meditated. This Guru Rinpoche cave is over a hundred miles from the Tibetan border, at Tso.Pema (Lotus Lake) in northern India.*

Opposite *Ferrymen were common in Tibet, because although Tibetans took the art of building suspension bridges across deep ravines to great heights (literally!), the volume of traffic across the broader rivers of the plains seldom justified the expense of building a bridge.*

40

matter), and this was true regardless of rank. Women took little part in the ruling of the country, but then, no one took much part in the ruling of Tibet: government was minimal. It was well known in Lhasa which wives influenced their husbands, and one unfortunate gentleman who held an administrative post of some importance was both admired and pitied for the way in which he refused the bribes which supplicants brought to him at the suggestion of his own wife.

Among the poor, it was not necessarily expected that a girl would bring her virginity to the marriage bed; what she did before she was married was her concern. Customs varied from place to place, though, so that a Khamba will say of a girl who is free with her favours, "She's a real Amdowa, that one!" though Amdowas deny the charge vociferously. Among the rich, virginity was expected (though by no means essential), but marriage contracts were drawn up on the express basis that if the couple should split up, they would each retain the property they had brought to the union. Furthermore, upper-class Tibetans had an attitude to marriage and divorce (which were purely secular matters) which is reminiscent of the ancient Romans: they would cheerfully divorce each other, and marry someone else, remaining the best of friends the whole while, so there was no great incentive for adultery.

One thing which intrigues many people about Tibetan society is the question of polygyng and polyandry. The simple truth is that many marriages in Tibet were arranged (though love-matches were by no means unknown), and that both polygyny and polyandry were based more on economics than

The original caption to this photograph from the collection of His Holiness the Dalai Lama indicates the cosmopolitan (if sometimes unexpected) tastes of the Tibetan aristocracy: 'Governor of Lower Kham, his wife, and Piper. Tibetans have adopted the Scottish bagpipes as their national instrument. [Not true – RWH]. They can play "Cock of the North", "The Campbells are Coming", and "The Drunken Piper", having learned their music in India.'

Both the Potala and the Chakpori medical school can be seen in this picture taken across the Lhasa plain in the spring.

on libido. Usually, two or three sisters might marry one man, or two or three brothers marry one girl, in order not to split up a family estate. Women could inherit as well as men, so two sisters might consider it better to stay together, and marry just one man, than to go their own ways and lose their security. 'Group' marriages seem never to have taken place, with two or more brothers marrying two or more sisters; normally, family alliances would be better served by one man marrying one or two sisters, and the other sisters marrying someone else. There were a few plural marriages which were not of siblings, but they were rare, and normally took place only among the very rich.

Although women were not normally educated to the same standard as men, there was by no means a ban on such education; one Khamba girl explained how, as an only child, she was "both daughter and son to my parents", who took her to Lhasa for an education. Fortunately, the move to Lhasa had some sort of stimulating effect, and her parents had the additional children they wanted, but still they did not stint on Rinchen-la's education. It may even be that their dedication to their daughter's education saved all their lives, because in 1959 they went to Mussoorie in India to enrole her in a boarding school, and while they were there Tibet rose against the Chinese and the Dalai Lama fled Lhasa: they have never been back. At the time of writing, Rinchen-la's sister was just completing medical school in India. Khambas, incidentally, are regarded as the most headstrong of Tibetans; Amdowas are regarded as peaceful farmers; and Tsangpas are the butt of jokes, just as the Irish are in England and the Poles in America.

43

A Tibetan joke against Tsangpas illustrates how the Tibetan sense of humour works; it is frequently (one might say normally) robust to the extent of coarseness, but it does not always translate: this one does.

A nobleman, wishing to impress an important visitor, calls for his Tsangpa servant and asks him to prepare a horse for him to ride after the meeting, so that he can relax. "Certainly, sir," says the Tsangpa, "do you want one with a prick or without a prick?" The master, scandalised, yells at him to get out. He goes and sits on the kitchen step, very miserable, wondering what he has done wrong. As he is sitting there, the picture of dejection, a friend of his who is a nun walks past. "What's the matter?" she says. He tells her the story. "Oh, you fool," she says, "the words are *stallion* and *mare*. Now go back and ask him again." He goes back in, and asks his master if he wants a stallion or a mare. The visitor has gone, and the business went well, so the master is in a good mood. He tells the servant not to bother about the horse, but says how pleased he is that the servant has taken the trouble to find out the right words. "Oh, it was nothing," says the servant. "This friend of mine told me. She's a monk without a prick..."

To return to everyday life in Tibet (though it must be said that jokes are a part of everyday life in Tibet, and that this was one of the cleaner ones), life was not all work. It is easy to forget that although subsistence farming does require hard work, and although it does not provide a materially high standard of living, it also involves a good deal of leisure time and waiting for the crops to grow. The usual occupations were sitting around, talking, joking, drinking tea and chang, and playing dice. Many Tibetans are inveterate gamblers; anyone who thinks that this is a Western vice should sit in on a game of dice or cards at Losar, the Tibetan New Year celebrations.

There were many high days and holidays, part religious, and part secular. The pattern would have been familiar to our mediaeval ancestors in the West: a visit to the temple for a religious ceremony in the morning, perhaps as early as dawn, and then a fair, a play or some sort of sports in the afternoon. Losar was the archetypal festival; the first month of the Tibetan year begins in February or March, because the Tibetan calendar is lunar, and the exact date is therefore variable.

After the religious ceremony at dawn on the first day of the new year, the custom was to visit close friends and relatives to drink Losar chang, rather like the Scots ceremony of 'first footing'; on subsequent days, the circle of people to visit widened steadily, and parties (rather than family gather-

ings) were the order of the day. In theory, Losar celebrations last three days; in practice, they would often last until the fifteenth day of the first month, especially in Lhasa where party going was a fine art. During the festivities, there would be dancing, athletics, and a good deal of drinking.

Tibetan dancing is very much a communal affair. Typically, the men and the women form into two long lines. They may dance facing one another, or in a circle, or in a single long line, and there is an accompanying song which is sung in alternate verses by the men and the women. The actual dances are mostly slow and foot-stamping, but some are very fast and intricate, somewhat resembling a Scottish reel. The dancers are inclined to fortify themselves with chang before the dances, and to refresh themselves with more chang between dances, so sparkling eyes and a good deal of merriment are characteristic of the whole performance. There may be a fiddler to provide music, but more often the song is the sole accompaniment. The sound, rising and falling, can be heard over large distances, and as the evening waxes, the music and the dances become louder and faster.

Although every village had its own celebrations, both religious and secular (for weddings etc.), Tibetan social life was to be seen at its height in the towns; and most of all in Lhasa. Pilgrimages, in old Tibet as in mediaeval England, were the only holidays for most people, and Lhasa was also a centre for pilgrimage. So the Losar celebrations were joined in not only by all the regular city-dwellers, but also by pilgrims who had come from all over the country. In a motorised age, it is easy to forget how far you can walk in a day, or a week, and pilgrimages which involved several months' journey were by no means unusual; some took over a year! The pilgrims would be fed *en route* by complete strangers, whose generosity enabled them to share in the merit which the pilgrims themselves accumulated by making the pilgrimage, and also provided them with a welcome source of news and variety in a life which could otherwise be somewhat monotonous.

One of the major attractions at Losar was the variety of sports and parades organised in Lhasa. There were displays of arms and armour, an echo of Tibet's military greatness a thousand years ago: some of the armour was actually original, stored in the Potala for just this occasion. By edict of the Great Fifth Dalai Lama, an essential part of the Losar festivities was a display of the *Rinchen Gyan-cha*, or Precious Ornaments of

Martial sports, such as picking up **katags** *or hoops and then hitting the target first with a rifle and then with a bow and arrow, all from the back of a galloping horse, were standard entertainment at the post-Losar celebrations in Lhasa.*

Lhamo *folk operas were another popular entertainment, a tradition which is now kept alive in exile by the Tibetan Institute of Performing Arts in Dharamsala.*

Tsampa *(barley flour) is thrown in the air as an auspicious act in many ceremonies; here it is a part of the purification of the stage at a* Lhamo *performance.*

the Great Kings, though the historical authenticity of some of the ornaments themselves is uncertain. There were some surprisingly martial sports, indicating the similarities between Mongol and Tibetan culture. Horsemen armed with both guns and bows and arrows would shoot at two targets in quick succession, once with each weapon, from the back of a galloping horse; others, armed with long lances, would pick up *katags* from the ground – a matter of very fine judgement, as an inch too high would miss the target, but an inch too low would unseat the rider.

There were less martial games, too. Weight-lifting was one favourite: standard stones, kept from year to year for the games, were the weights. Often, instead of just lifting them, contestants had to carry them for a specified distance. There were foot-races, and two kinds of horse racing: the conventional kind, with riders, and an endearingly Tibetan variety in which the horses were raced without riders, along a marked and cleared course.

Life in Lhasa, the Big City, was of course different from life in the villages. To begin with, there were many innkeepers, restaurateurs, and shopkeepers, servicing the visitors to whom Lhasa was host. There were also large numbers of servants, because few Tibetan aristocrats spent much time on the estates from which they derived their income; instead, they lived in Lhasa, where they were required to render service in the Government. A well-to-do aristocrat might regularly employ as many as a dozen 'chang-girls', whose job it was to serve chang to his guests at parties and dinners. The Tibetan tradition is always to top up a guest's glass as soon as there is room, so these girls had a full-time job (and the guests rapidly lost track of the amount of chang they had consumed!).

Lhasa was also the home of the rising middle class, but they were never numerous and had no particular political importance. Modelling themselves on the gentry, in the historical pattern of most emergent middle classes, they were their own worst enemy: it was they who had the most to gain from modernisation and change, but they resisted it because the rich, who stood to lose most, resisted it.

A resistance to change was one of the most salient points of Tibetan culture – and it still is, to a certain extent – something that the Dalai Lama deprecates to this day. The aristocracy resisted change; the middle class resisted change; the peasants resisted change. But there was another class which was an even stronger defender of Tibetan tradition. This was, of course, the monks.

It was a matter of pride for most families to have at least one son in a monastery, and although it may seem strange to Western eyes to send a boy of six or seven to a monastery, it becomes easier to understand when the monastery is seen as a school as well as a religious institution. Life for a young Tibetan monk was not all that much different from life for a boy at an old-fashioned English boarding school: the routines and hierarchy would be familiar to either, though in England there would be more emphasis on games, and in Tibet more emphasis on religion.

Boys might be admitted to the monastery at a very tender age, and orphans might join as early as three or four if they had, say, an uncle who was a monk and who was prepared to look after them. They could (and still can) take the *Getsul* (preliminary) vows as young as seven, but they were not allowed to take the *Gelong* (final) vows until they were twenty – though not all monks take the Gelong vows, and although both sets of vows are binding, both can be set aside. This was and is not common, but nor is it particularly unusual: many monks in their twenties or thirties might choose to return to the lay community, and it was also quite usual for a layman to enter a monastery after a career outside. And as for admitting children to the monastic community, Jesus Christ made several remarks about the spiritual capabilities of children, and Our Lady of Fatima provides another example, where the Blessed Virgin appeared not to adults, but to children. Given the close interrelationship of everyday life with religion, the step from the lay community to the *Sangha* was not necessarily a large one; and by the same token, monks were a common sight in the community, as teachers, administrators, doctors, and priests.

Because of the sheer size of the monasteries, there was a considerable degree of diversification and specialisation among the monks – and the three great monasteries of Sera, Ganden, and Drepung near Lhasa could boast nearly 20,000 monks between them. The great ceremonies inside the monastery would usually be attended by all, high and low, but for the rest of the time, each had his own duties. There were monk-cooks, monk-treasurers, monk-police, monk-scholars and monk-teachers, and even monk-servants, looking after senior monks.

There is no doubt that the Tibetan monastic system had its faults. Everyone, including the Dalai Lama, agrees that there were far too many monks, especially those who just drifted into the monasteries as a result of tradition, parental pressure,

As in the West in mediaeval times, the monastic life offered (and still offers) a path for advancement and literacy, as well as for spiritual development.

or lack of any clear idea of what else to do. Some of the young monk-students had the same reputation as the undergraduates of mediaeval European universities (which were, of course, also religious institutions), with fraternities, boisterousness, and a degree of wildness which it is hard to square with any monastic tradition. There were also a few administrators who exploited their position for their own benefit, but overall the great monasteries also had many good points. They may have put a brake on material progress, but their grasp of the Buddhist science of the mind was unsurpassed.

Many of the stories of mystical powers which are told are pure fiction, but others are certainly true. The *Tumo* yoga of psychic heat control is a well-known example: there really were tests in which monks sat in icy caves, stark naked, and dried out sheets which had been soaked in tubs of glacial water. It must be added that heat production is merely incidental to the religious practice involved, though this is another matter. Similarly, there really were *lung-gom* runners who could run apparently tirelessly for hours on end – but once again, this was incidental to the religious practice involved, and, contrary to popular belief, lung-gom runners were not employed to carry messages between monasteries. Even the tales of conjuring up demons and apparitions are sometimes true: Tibetan Buddhism accepts that such things are illusory, but does not necessarily distinguish betweeen them and the illusion of the 'real' world.

There was also a good deal of practical learning carried on at the monastic universities. Medicine was advanced, even if the language used was flowery and old fashioned: 'Precious Purified Moon-Crystal Pills' may sound like mumbo-jumbo, but there was a strong theoretical and experimental clinical basis on which they were (and are) prescribed, and it is impossible to deny that they do work for some conditions and some people. It is also worth remembering that ornate names for chemicals survived in England well into the twentieth century: how about 'Lunar Caustic' (silver nitrate) or 'Flowers of Sulphur'?

The problem with much of the practical learning was, however, that it had tended to fossilise and fall into disuse. There are Tibetan treatises on surgery which are centuries old, and which look a good deal more likely to succeed than any Western surgery before the early-to-mid nineteenth century, but surgery was hardly practised at all in Tibet at any time in this century. Of course, it is a fair criticism that by neglecting the practical side of things, the monks were

Dob-Dobs, or monk-police, were recruited from the biggest and fiercest monks. Some used to blacken their faces with soot to make themselves look even more ferocious.

51

being un-Buddhist: the Buddha himself always advocated the value of the Middle Path. Nevertheless, the loss of the monasteries of Tibet, and the loss of their libraries and much of their learning, has been one of the great losses of the twentieth century, even if they did bring it upon themselves by their intransigence and opposition to all change, even when change was instigated by the Dalai Lama himself.

We have already mentioned the aristocracy, and now it is time to look at them in more detail. The aristocracy was at once clearly ranked, and curiously ill defined, as well as being much more flexible than might be imagined. Above everyone was the Dalai Lama and (when applicable) the Regent, and then came the six *Yab-shi* families, including the family of the present Dalai Lama – who were raised to that estate from being very modest farmers in a remote part of Amdo. When their son was recognised as the true Incarnation, his parents were automatically elevated to the peerage, to ranks which might in European terms be equated to Duke and Duchess. The present Dalai Lama's father was a man of simple tastes, who spent much of his time with his horses, and the Great Mother or *Gyalyum Chhenmo* could only with difficulty be

The Yab-Shi, *or Royal Family: the Great Mother and father of the Fourteenth Dalai Lama, with their two younger children. On the left is Mrs Pema Gyalpo (as she now is), and on the right is Tendzing Choegyal, Ngari Rinpoche.*

Time and again, the beauty of Tibet as shown in these old and time-faded Kodachromes brought a lump to my throat as I thought of what the Tibetans have lost.

persuaded to wear the silk robes which were expected of her: under them, she wore simple peasant-style dress. The rest of the family was also ennobled, and to this day the nieces and nephews of His Holiness are called princes and princesses.

The Lha-gyari family occupy an anomalous position, as descendants of the ancient Kings, and are regarded as akin to Yab-shi.

After the Yab-shi came the four *de-pon* families, the Do-gar (Rakashar), the Do-ring (Gab-shi), the Thon-pa, and the Sam-pho, though not everyone includes the Sam-pho family, which means that they count only three de-pon. The third rank consisted of the fifteen *mi-drag* families, and then came the rest of the aristocracy.

Given the possibility that the greatest in the land might come from very humble beginnings, it is not surprising that the aristocracy was also, to a large extent, a meritocracy. Poor but intelligent and hard-working officials might expect rapid advancement, whereas scions of old and well-established families who did not pull their weight might fade away from the Lhasa scene, or even return to their estates. Actual demotion was rare, but even that was changing: both the Great Thirteenth and the Fourteenth Dalai Lamas had plans for replacing the old system, whereby officials were granted lands in return for government work, with a modern system of graded salaries. Still more radically, the land that was thus freed would have been redistributed among the peasants who actually worked it. Had this plan been successful, hereditary offices would have declined dramatically and a modern civil service might have resulted, but both Dalai Lamas were frustrated in their plans. The Great Thirteenth was blocked by the monasteries, and by the general inertia of the times, and the present Dalai Lama was blocked by the Chinese, because it would have robbed them of their 'justification' for invasion. They had, after all, come to 'liberate the peasants from Western Imperialism, serf-owning aristocrats, and the reactionary Dalai clique'. Given that there were no 'Western imperialists', and that the 'reactionary Dalai clique' was trying to give the peasants the land and diminish the power of the 'serf-owning imperialists', their case looked distinctly weak.

As well as the aristocracy, there were several old families of no particular aristocratic pretensions who provided a steady stream of administrators and who were regarded in much the same way as the old English 'squirearchy' or landed gentry: adjectives such as 'good', 'reliable', and 'well-established' were uttered approvingly.

As a result of all this, Tibetan aristocracy, government, and high society presented a very mixed picture. Most were receptive to new ideas, but a few clung to the old ways. Some of the newer members were concerned to preserve their own social standing, whereas the older families tended to be quietly confident. There was a certain amount of in-fighting among the ambitious, which could become serious if the Dalai Lama was not firmly in control: during the minority of the present Dalai Lama, the various factions supporting the two Regents who were appointed in turn were sometimes very badly behaved; even monasteries were not sacrosanct, and at least one library was burned and destroyed.

None of this affected the ordinary people very much, because their lives remained much the same whoever was in power, but it did mean that there was an instability and lack of continuity at the top of Tibetan society which the Chinese could and did exploit. The underlying culture was always uniquely Tibetan, and the biggest single cultural import was of course Buddhism from India, but there was also a significant Chinese influence, especially among the better-off, who would frequently use Chinese silks and porcelain, and employ Chinese cooks and even gardeners. The Chinese use this as one of the bases of their claims for suzerainty over Tibet, but their argument is about as strong as a French claim to rule England on the basis that well-to-do Englishmen have always enjoyed French wine and have (when they could afford it)

In many areas of Tibet, water-powered mills are common but here the suspended pestle allows a surprisingly easy action in the mortar. Barley was commonly ground in this way, to make tsampa.

54

Colonel Younghusband's expedition to Tibet was really an invasion – but his honesty, straightforwardness, and refusal to shed blood unnecessarily laid the foundations of Anglo-Tibetan friendship.

hired French chefs. In any case, Manchu influence was waning rapidly at the time of the accession of the Great Thirteenth Dalai Lama, and being replaced by Western influences from the British Raj in India.

In 1904, the British sent an expeditionary force into Tibet, to negotiate a treaty whereby the Tibetan government would undertake not to deal with any other major power – by which the British meant Russia, because these were the closing stages of the Great Game in Central Asia. As we have already seen, the Dalai Lama fled to Mongolia, and when he returned, he found that the Manchus had not only completely failed to help the Tibetans eject the British, but had also mounted an invasion of their own. He was forced to flee again: but this time, he went to British India.

It may seem extraordinary that he should seek refuge in a country occupied by a nation which only a few years before had invaded his own land, but the Tibetans have a saying that once you have experienced the scorpion, the frog seems friendly. The frog, with its bulging eyes, threatening appearance, and sudden moves, is a symbol of aggression in Tibet, but it is nothing like as deadly as the stealthy scorpion. The British frog had shown restraint during the invasion: Colonel Younghusband, the leader, had been careful to avoid unnecessary bloodshed, and of course had not permitted atrocities, looting, or wanton destruction. Furthermore, the British had announced their intention to invade, and the purpose of their invasion; they had invaded; and once they had secured their purpose, they had withdrawn. The Chinese had concealed their plans, and showed every sign of staying. The British seemed a safer bet.

In the event, the British proved surprisingly reticent. They were not willing to become too involved in Tibet, on the understandable grounds that it was too big and too unprofitable to police – though if the surveyor they had sent in had paid more attention to his brief, and less to his hobby of amateur naturalist, their verdict might have been different. Nevertheless, Sir Charles Bell proved an honest advisor to the Great Thirteenth, and the deaths in quick succession of the Son of Heaven and his dowager mother enabled the Tibetan people to throw the Manchus out unaided, amid the general collapse of the Celestial Empire. The Dalai Lama returned to Tibet in 1913, and formally reasserted Tibetan independence; therafter, he looked increasingly to the West.

A strong faction of the aristocracy followed his lead, albeit superficially in many cases. Western imports became a fad: the fedora hat became almost a part of the Tibetan national costume, and such imports as guns were very popular: the Yab-shi was not alone in having a Bren gun in the basement. There was no form of arms control in old Tibet, and bullets were sold alongside butter in the marketplace. Watches were another great favourite: to this day, you will find gentle and holy monks who are apparently completely indifferent to worldly affairs and worldly possessions – except for an extremely impressive watch. Then, as now, these magnificent timepieces were set to a rough approximation of the time, and three friends might find that their watches differed by as

Sir Charles Bell became a close and trusted adviser of the Great Thirteenth Dalai Lama, who greatly admired the British, even if he did not always trust their imperial manoeuverings.

Bullets – especially .303 bullets – were sold beside butter in the Lhasa markets: there was no form of arms control in the old Tibet.

much as a quarter of an hour or so. By the 1940s and 1950s, imports came both from the West and from Russia and China (who were on speaking terms in those days), and included both small things like electric flashlights and vacuum flasks and quite major items such as motorcycles – there was no way to get cars into Tibet in any significant numbers, because of the vast distances and terrible roads, to say nothing of problems with the availability of fuel. There was no driving test of any sort, nor any insurance, or any other sort of bureaucracy or preparation, and more than one motorcycle (and motorcyclist) was wrecked on the first ride. A friend's father, in Kham, was travelling between two villages when he lost his pillion passenger without noticing. When he realised that he had dumped his farm manager somewhere on the track, he went back: the unfortunate passenger was quite unhurt, and kept apologising profusely for his carelessness and stupidity in falling off!

Extremely fine jewellery was produced in Tibet, and even today it is possible (though not easy) to find workmanship very much better than the usual run of tourist brooches. Techniques have changed very little, except that centrifugal blowers are now used for less delicate work, and the jewellers no longer wear such formal dress.

Opposite above Despite the fact that Heinrich Harrer's book Seven Years In Tibet *made him more famous than Peter Aufschnaiter, it seems clear that Aufschnaiter accomplished a great deal constructing dams, roads, and other public works.*

Opposite below In addition to his engineering work, Aufschnaiter did a good deal of surveying, and this photograph was probably taken on one of his surveying trips.

Although this gives the lie of the stories of 'reactionary' Tibetans, and shows that the lack of wheeled transport in Tibet was almost entirely a matter of practicality, it does not tell the whole story. Unfortunately, Tibetans were less willing to adopt Western ways where they mattered, notably in education and defence. The attempts of the Great Thirteenth to introduce Western-style schools were shunned. The four boys who went to Rugby school in the 1920s were never followed by others, because parents would not volunteer their children. Attempts to modernise the army were continually frustrated by the refusal of young men of good family to join an officer corps, and by a chronic shortage of suitable men for the ranks. The Great Thirteenth wanted to draft monks, but the monasteries predictably opposed that. When the Great Thirteenth died in 1933, things simply drifted until the Fourteenth came to power; but by then, it was too late.

Tibet met all the usual criteria for independence, including issuing coinage and postage stamps. A somewhat stylised snow lion forms the centrepiece of this stamp.

The Dalai Lama was surrouunded with such a wall of formality that it was extremely difficult even to catch a glimpse of him when (as here) he was carried from the Potala which served as a winter palace to the Norbulingka or summer palace.

Below *The modernised Tibetan army, set up in the 1920s, was always handicapped by the unwillingness of aristocratic families to allow their sons to become officers, and by the very stiff protocol governing personal (as distinct from military) rank in Tibet.*

If only...This photograph shows the 1948 Tibetan Trade Mission, which could have been the first stage towards a modern and industrialising Tibetan state, if only the Chinese had not invaded less than two years later.

The aristocracy went on, therefore, in their own sweet way, untroubled by the realisation that their world was doomed. They still had things made in the old way, bringing the craftsmen (weavers, silversmiths, or whatever) into their own houses, and paying for their food while they worked. They still administered their estates, and the country, as though the Great Fifth Dalai Lama was still in power, and they surrounded the office of Dalai Lama with an ever more stifling barrier of protocol and etiquette. The monasteries were equally blinkered, cutting themselves deeper and deeper grooves of ritual. The fall of Tibet was all but inevitable.

79 10

OCCUPIED TIBET

Ordinary narration breaks down in the face of the Chinese occupation of Tibet. The scale of exploitation and destruction is too great: all that can be recounted are episodes and fragments.

Individual stories and assertions are hard to prove. The Tibetans say that over a million of their countrymen have perished since the Chinese invasion – many from fighting the Chinese, but many more from starvation, persecution or political purges. Given that an American government report (the Warren committee) put the number of people killed in Mao's China in the years 1949-71 at between 32 and 64 million this does not seem unlikely. The individual stories of hardships and atrocities are sufficiently numerous, and sufficiently well corroborated, that in 1960 the International Commission of Jurists found that there was a *prima facie* case of genocide against the Chinese in Tibet. There are endless photographs of the destruction of monasteries, the defacement of religious images, and the use of *mani* stones bearing sacred inscriptions as paving stones in toilets. Perhaps the strongest proof lies in the number of Tibetan refugees who have fled the country; over one hundred thousand, or one Tibetan in sixty. Many of them bear the bullet-scars that they acquired during their escape; many also bear stories of those who tried to escape with them, but failed. And every single refugee that you meet has come out since 1950.

And yet, there are still many people in the West who believe the Chinese version of the invasion: that the Tibetans were oppressed by reactionary feudal lords and an idle and corrupt priesthood, presided over by a Dalai Lama who was concerned only for his own comfort – and who, eventually, fled only to save his own skin. The Chinese propaganda machine is strong, Tibet is a long way off, and there are plenty of better-documented wars and atrocities than the Chinese invasion of Tibet: in a media age, mere words cannot compete with photographs and television.

But there are photographs, though they have not been widely published. The majority were taken by members of the various delegations sent into Tibet by the Dalai Lama. They were not taken by professional photographers, and in the nature of things, they are one-sided: they do not show everyone dressed in the suspiciously new and clean clothes that always seem to appear in Chinese propaganda pictures, even on the backs of agricultural labourers and road gangs; people are dressed in patched and darned old *chubas*. They do not show the magnificent new factories which the Chinese always extol; instead, they show that many of these 'factories' are no more than back-street workshops by Western standards. They do not show new Chinese buildings: they show ruined monasteries and defaced religious statues. They do not show roads, at least not in any Western sense – just quagmires through which four-wheel-drive vehicles can pass only with difficulty.

There are many other things which they do not show. There are no photographs of the political prisons, in which thousands or perhaps tens of thousands of Tibetans are held. There are no photographs of the devastation caused by Chinese nuclear weapon tests in Tibet. There are no photographs of the appalling pollution for which some Chinese factories are responsible, nor do they show that other factories lie idle for most of the year, because they were built to satisfy

Above left Most of the much-vaunted 'roads' built by the Chinese in Tibet (with Tibetan forced labour) are like this: quagmires suitable only for four-wheel drive vehicles in dry weather.

Above centre and right The 'factories' are often little more than back-yard workshops. This is true throughout the developing world, of course, but it is easy for Westerners to forget.

Opposite Ruins framed in ruins: the remains of Shekar Dzong after Chinese bombing and shelling.

64

some bureaucratic plan or to impress a visiting party dignitary, without any consideration of the availability of raw materials or power. They do not show the public executions, the forced sterilisations, the Tibetan children raiding Chinese dustbins for food, the schools used as lumber stores.

What they do show, however, is that there is still hope in Tibet. Everywhere the members of the delegations went, they were besieged by hundreds or thousands of people. Everyone in the delegations was asked to distribute blessings in the name of the Dalai Lama, but when they protested that they were lay-people, and could not give blessings, the entreaties began again. They were also begged to give names to children: the custom in old Tibet was to ask a high lama for a name for a child, but since all the lamas had been killed or imprisoned, there had been no one to ask, and a whole generation had been brought up with makeshift names – the day of the week they were born, the name of the month, or the season. There was no way that the delegates could refuse to give names, and they handed out names all over Tibet! Anyone who appeared in the name of His Holiness was sanctified by his mandate.

When the Chinese first invaded, their impact was nothing like as bad as had been feared. The discipline in the communist army was far greater than that of previous invaders: these soldiers had been told to confine themselves to military objectives, and that there were to be no reprisals against civilians.

Some idea of the crowds that besieged the Delegation can be gained from this picture which was taken from the roof of the Jokhang. The iron gates (seen just above the parapet) were later opened.

Compare the finish and condition of this 'propaganda' chuba and hat with the appearance of the children. They would not normally appear in Chinese propaganda shots.

79 10 8

For the most part they followed these orders to the letter. But the Tibetans who fought against them soon saw the scant regard which the Chinese had for human life: they would use the bodies of the dead and wounded as sandbags to build emplacements, their own men as well as Tibetans.

The Tibetans could also see what 'equality' meant in the Chinese communist army. Senior officers were equipped with oxygen bottles, but junior officers and other ranks were left to manage as best they could. Given that they were fighting at altitudes of two *miles* and more, they must have suffered terribly: normally, it takes months to acclimatise to such altitude. No wonder the Tibetans often inflicted Chinese casualties ten or even twenty times greater than Tibetan losses. As Mao Tse-Tung was to say many years later, "China is not afraid to lose a million men in a war". A Chinese general, speaking in the late 1950s, showed the same disregard for humanity when he said, "We do not care what the Tibetan people want. We can always draft in enough soldiers to make them do what *we* want."

In the early years after the invasion, the Chinese persisted in propagating the myth that they were there at the request of the Tibetan people, and that they would leave as soon as Tibet was able to govern itself – an odd proviso, in the light of the fact that Tibet had been doing just that until the Chinese invaded. But many of the Chinese soldiers seem sincerely to have believed it, and the conflict between what they had been told and what they could see for themselves was immense.

The First Delegation to Tibet in 1979. His Holiness's elder brother, Lobsang Samten, is the man at the front, with the Panchen Lama behind him; Phuntsog Wangyal (a long-time Party member) is on the extreme right.

Each resolved it in his own way, as soldiers have always done. Some withdrew further into themselves; some busied themselves in the military life; and some even went over to the Tibetan side. One of the most senior to do so was an artillery commander, Chang Ho-ther; he was given the Tibetan name of Losang Tashi, and fought alongside the Tibetans until after His Holiness had escaped to India. He now lives in the Tibetan settlement at Bylakuppe, in south India.

Basically, though, the differences between the invaders and the invaded were irreconcilable. One of the most fundamental differences lay in their attitudes to religion: the Chinese, as hard-line Marxists, saw it as reactionary and oppressive, while the devoutly Buddhist Tibetans saw it as progressive and liberating. The Chinese made no attempt to understand Tibetan spirituality: the Tibetans made very little attempt to understand Chinese materialism. The attitude of both sides is perfectly comprehensible: the Chinese in the army had, for the most part, benefited from communism, while the Tibetans had almost all seen a decline in their own living standards because of it. The presence of a huge garrison in Lhasa – six thousand men in mid-1951, and another seven or eight thousand a few months later – reduced the Tibetan poor to near-starvation as food prices soared, and the monasteries could offer no help because their stocks had all been requisitioned.

Even where there was a measure of agreement between the Tibetans and the Chinese, the Chinese would only allow things to be done their way. For example, the Dalai Lama

Chang Ho-Ther was a Chinese artillery commander until he went over to the Tibetan side, where he was given the name Losang Tashi. This picture was taken in a Tibetan refugee camp in South India.

Only traces remain of the bright and ornate paintwork which once covered this temple door in Ba-Kham, now that it is used as a store-house.

79 10 7

Tibet is not an infertile country, as this picture from Shigatse shows – but it cannot feed a limitless number of Chinese immigrants. Note the incongruously new chubas *being worn for field work – a sure sign that the scene has been set up by the Chinese.*

wished to continue the process started by the Great Thirteenth, whereby government officials would be paid a salary in lieu of giving them estates, which could then be redistributed among the peasants who actually farmed the land. The Chinese were equally against large landlords, but clung rigidly to the doctrine of collectivisation rather than individual ownership – and there were, of course, powerful forces in Tibet who wished to preserve the *status quo*, for their own good.

Predictably, the Chinese 'negotiations' for 'progressive improvements' made no headway. In the early 1950s, although they were theoretically trying to impose their will peacefully, they were so heavy-handed that they might as well have resorted to violence. For example, they habitually stationed armed guards outside His Holiness's door during talks, and the personal behaviour of the Chinese generals who were supposed to be negotiating was such that the Dalai

71

Lama accepted the resignations of his two Prime Ministers rather than endanger them by allowing them to come into constant conflict with the Chinese. Their actual resignation was prompted by Chinese demands for the removal of Lukhangwa, the lay Prime Minister, who opposed them consistently and with reasoned arguments, but who was accused (not unreasonably) of not wishing to improve relations between Tibet and China.

In 1954, the Chinese invited the Dalai Lama to visit China. Many Tibetans were against this, fearing they would never see him again, but His Holiness believed the journey should be made, because he might have some chance of influencing the Chinese leadership. Treated royally, he met Mao Tse-tung and Chou En-lai; although they promised investigations of 'mistakes' made by Chinese officials in Tibet, there were no changes: in fact, the reliance on force, which the Chinese had been using in Kham and Amdo from the very start, slowly began to appear in Lhasa too.

The Chinese did, however, persuade His Holiness to agree to act as Chairman of the Preparatory Committee for the Autonomous Region of Tibet. The brief hopes which this

Once the disastrous attempts to regulate farming according to Mao Tse-Tung Thought were abandoned, Tibet began to produce barley once more in very respectable quantities – though a good deal goes to China in 'taxes', and more is used to feed Chinese 'advisers' and 'technicians' whose advice and techniques the Tibetans can easily do without.

72

aroused in him were soon dashed when it became clear that the Autonomous Region of Tibet was a truncated country, shorn of the rich Eastern provinces of Kham and Amdo (which the Chinese claimed as part of China). In any case, the Committee was both heavily loaded with Chinese sympathisers (as well as five Chinese) over whose appointment he had no control and was also expected to act as a rubber stamp for decisions already made by the local Communist Party Committee (which contained no Tibetans at all). For the ordinary Tibetan people, life was becoming increasingly harsh. Restrictions on movement were becoming more and more onerous; food was becoming ever scarcer and more expensive; and Chinese brutality and aggression were becoming more and more widespread.

Initially, many Tibetans had not been fully aware of the implications of the Chinese invasion, but the mere fact that their country was being overrun prompted many who were immediately affected to fight. When the Chinese began impos-

The Kashag or Tibetan cabinet, from whose files this picture came, know nothing about the subject or where it was taken; but once again, it is the recurring symbol of the man with the horse and the gun, in a vast landscape. The Tibetan dream comes surprisingly close to the American west sometimes.

ing intolerable rules and regulations, and particularly when they tried to suppress the Tibetan religion, more and more Tibetans were provoked into physical retaliation and the formation of a resistance movement.

No one is sure when the first really horrific incidents occurred: Chinese restrictions on movement, and Tibetan imprecision about exact dates, ensured that exact details are hard to find. But there is no doubt that some hideous things happened. For example, in one village where the village council refused to accept collectivisation, the twenty-four leading men of the village were tied to stakes, doused in petrol, and burned alive. In another instance, the teenage daughters of recalcitrant farmers were rounded up, stripped naked, and marched at gun-point through the village, past jeering Chinese in the military camp, and into a shallow lake of icy water. They were made to stand there all day: at least they were not raped, a fate which befell many of their sisters. The first large-scale response to these and similar atrocities was the Lithang uprising of 1 June 1956 – an uprising which the Chinese countered by bombing Lithang monastery.

Almost by definition, these things happened in the most out of the way places at first. In Lhasa, few stories filtered back, and those that did were unlikely to reach the ears of the Dalai Lama. It was only as His Holiness was returning

"Our first contact with the Khambas was when they invited Patterson to deal with a guerrilla whose foot had become gangrenous with frostbite. Before he first visited Tibet in the 1940s Patterson had had a nine-months "crash medical course" in an English hospital. He cut off the two toes with a razor blade tied on to a stick. The Khamba had no anaesthetic besides sleeping tablets and rice wine."

from the 2,500th Buddha Jayanti in India that he began to hear them, usually at second hand: no one who was not close to him would speak to the Dalai Lama of such matters. He heard the stories first in Darjeeling and Kalimpong, from the Tibetan traders who were based there and from the refugees who had swelled their numbers. Then, as he slowly returned to Lhasa early in 1957, he heard more and more. By the time he returned, he was under no illusions about what the Chinese were doing to his country.

Even then, he tried to avoid conflict – although, as he put it himself, he knew that for some people things really could not get any worse. What he was afraid of was a general Tibetan uprising, followed by Chinese retaliation on a scale which the Tibetans could not match. This would, he knew, be a bloodbath, so he constantly urged anyone who spoke of armed resistance to wait, to consider their actions, and to avoid shedding either Chinese or Tibetan blood. If he had not adopted this course, and if he had supported the Tibetan resistance movement in the way the Chinese accused him of doing, the Tibetan uprising would have started at least a year earlier, and the bloodshed might well have been worse.

The Chinese, meanwhile, were growing more and more arrogant. They had realised that they could impose their will only by force and were beginning to prepare themselves to use it. Furthermore, like any colonial administrators, power had gone to their heads. In China, they might be senior or even quite minor army officers: in Tibet, they were governors of large areas, with (literally) the power of life and death over their subjects. The literature of European colonialism is full of such examples, and Chinese colonialists were no different.

As early as 1955, there were organised cells of local resistance; by 1958, the resistance was organised at a national level. The only reason that there was not a full-scale insurrection was the moderating influence of the Dalai Lama, but there were many clashes and skirmishes by individual groups driven to desperation. Some were major military operations: local dzongs occupied by the Chinese would be overrun by Tibetan resistance fighters, and some strongpoints changed hands two or three times. Arms were scraped up from anywhere: some came from arsenals in monasteries, which had traditionally held the weapons of the local militia, and others were captured from the Chinese.

One of the great leaders of the Resistance, Gompo Tashi Andrugtsang was a successful merchant in middle years before leading the Chushi Gangdrug *against the Chinese. His autobiography,* Four Rivers, Six Ranges, *is a fascinating book.*

In 1959 the Chinese themselves precipitated matters by inviting the Dalai Lama to a concert in their barracks on 10 March, though it was not so much an invitation as a command. They stipulated that he should come without his usual bodyguard, that his retinue should be limited to 25, none of whom should be armed, that he should come without the usual ceremony, and that the Tibetan soldiers who normally lined his route should be confined to barracks. They had previously announced on Radio Peking that the Dalai Lama would be attending the National People's Congress (NPC) in Peking later that year – a conference which, it was well known he had been at pains to avoid agreeing to attend. They also made the almost impossible demand that the journey to the camp should be kept secret. When this became known, a crowd of some thirty thousand Tibetans surrounded his summer palace in the Norbulingka or Jewel Park, in order to prevent his going.

After some days of mounting tension and excitement, it became clear that the Chinese were going to use force: military surveyors were seen taking readings, apparently to align guns on the Palace; a message was sent warning the Dalai Lama and his entourage to shelter deep in the palace; and at four o'clock in the afternoon of 17 March, two mortar shells landed in a pond in the Norbulingka. Despite attempts by His Holiness's staff to disperse the crowd, there were still many thousands of people outside the Norbulingka, and the only realistic possibility was for him to try and escape.

The story of how the Dalai Lama escaped, disguised as a common soldier, is told both in his autobiography and in *Great Ocean*; for the present, it is enough to say that it was an epic journey through the Tibetan winter, and that he reached safety in India in early April – but not before he had formally repudiated the Seventeen-Point Agreement which had been foisted upon Tibet after the invasion, and reaffirmed his own government as the only legitimate government of Tibet. He did this at Lhuntse Dzong, the last major administrative centre before the Indian border.

Now that His Holiness was gone, there was nothing to restrain either the Tibetan resistance or Chinese retaliation. The Chinese shelled the Norbulingka and the crowd surrounding it, using mortars and heavy artillery at short range: the carnage was incredible. When they had finished with that target, they turned their guns on the monuments of Lhasa itself. They shelled the Jokhang, often referred to by Westerners as Lhasa's 'cathedral', the holiest temple in all of Tibet; they shelled Chakpori, the ancient monastic medical college; they shelled everything. Some parts escaped much more lightly than others, partly due to luck, but also due to the fortress-like nature of Tibetan architecture.

The legendary golden roofs of the Jokhang, the most sacred temple in all Tibet, often referred to by Western writers as Lhasa's 'cathedral'.

These almost shapeless lumps of rock, now recovered and respectfully wrapped with katags, *are the heads of once beautiful carved stone statues mutilated by the Chinese, but rescued by devout Tibetans and smuggled into India. They are now preserved as relics in the temple in Dharamsala.*

Outside Lhasa, the incidents which had hitherto been isolated atrocities became commonplace. Aged monks and nuns were yoked to the plough and used as draught animals, and flogged until they dropped. Other nuns were gang-raped, or forced at pistol-point to have intercourse with monks. Wives were raped in front of their husbands, daughters (including little girls) in front of their fathers; they might or might not be shot afterwards, depending on the whim of the soldiers. Men and women were shot in public, or even tortured to death publicly, as an example to anyone who might contemplate crossing the Chinese. Ancient tortures were revived from the days of the Celestial Empire, including flaying alive, slow burning, putting out of eyes, and driving chopsticks into the ears, and modern variants were added: a common punishment for freedom fighters, or for anyone suspected of 'reactionary' behaviour was to tie each arm and leg to a different jeep, and then drive off in four different directions.

Special venom was reserved for religion and its practice. Monks and nuns were always a prime target, but so were devout lay-people; they were forced to desecrate monasteries and destroy libraries, using *mani* stones (stones inscribed with prayers and religious texts) as flooring, especially in latrines, or lining shoes with religious texts. It was not merely a question of the destruction of religion: the losses to scholarship were also incalculable, because no more than a dozen copies of even a recent book might exist, while some libraries held thousand-year-old manuscripts copied from originals which no longer existed in India. It is not unrealistic to compare Chinese destruction of centres of learning in Tibet with the destruction of the library of Alexandria in AD 640; by comparison, the book-burning of the Inquisition or of the Nazis was the work of uncoordinated amateurs.

China itself was of course in turmoil. The Great Leap Forward had been a complete failure, and the Red Guards were now in the ascendant. The destruction had been terrible before they gained control; now it went beyond belief. The army had already dynamited many monasteries, on the grounds that some of them contained arsenals and were strongholds of the resistance, but a few had escaped, and the destruction was incomplete in others. Some soldiers had amused themselves by shooting at religious sculptures or paintings – their vandalism was nothing next to the work of the Red Guards, who systematically set out to destroy every vestige of religion. Where there was too much even for their energy, they desecrated it as best they could: rows of painted Buddhas on a wall, beautiful even to a non-Buddhist, would have their eyes scraped out in a labour of hate which would take many hours to complete, although if the Red Guards and the army tired of their destruction themselves, they could always force the Tibetans to do it at gunpoint.

The faces of all the images in this Tradug Dolma lhakhang have been carefully obliterated as a symbol of the Chinese communists' contempt for religion.

The Chinese also looted Tibet on an almost inconceivable scale. Many of the religious images in the temples were made of alloys rich in gold, or even of solid gold, and they were ornamented with precious and semi-precious stones. Sometimes, the stones were ripped from their settings and the statues melted down for bullion; a more common fate, where the bullion value was relatively low compared to the extrinsic worth of the sculptures, was removal to China for sale to the West via Hong Kong. In the 1960s an English antique dealer who was offering a surprising range of Tibetan ritual objects in his shop in Cornwall explained, "It's all a question of who you know. If you've got a quarter of a million [pounds], I can get you a solid gold Buddha." An accurate estimate of the value of the loot taken from Tibet would be impossible, but any estimate must run into billions of American dollars.

Nor was it a question of Chinese violence being directed against a few 'reactionaries and counter-revolutionaries', as the Chinese would maintain. In those days, almost anything was enough to classify someone as a 'reactionary'. A typical

In a courtyard of the Norbulingka. Statues made of precious metal were melted for bullion: others, some over a thousand years old, were stamped flat and taken for scrap.

example might be a preference for Tibetan clothes instead of the Mao jacket and blue trousers which formed the Chinese uniform; another might be a muttered oath after a stubbed toe. "Kunchog sum!" is a common Tibetan exclamation, which literally means "Three jewels!", but the 'Three jewels' are the Lord Buddha, the Dharma or body of teaching, and the Sangha or community of monks. Or, of course, the leader of the thamzing sessions might simply not like you, whether for personal or political reasons.

Thamzing, or 'mutual self-criticism', was central to old-style Maoism. The self-critical element was notably absent from party members, except insofar as they pledged ever-greater support for the Party, and ever-greater efforts to root out 'imperialists, reactionaries, and aristocrats'. More to the point for most people was the 'mutual' part, in which the short-comings of others were denounced. The accused were then expected to grovel before the group, begging forgiveness for their shortcomings and thanking the Party for looking after them and correcting their ways, even though they were utterly unworthy.

The scope for abuse was obviously enormous, and it was fully exploited. Because thamzing sessions operated in a basically hysterical manner, there was no need for evidence or proof; old scores could be settled, and previously important figures humiliated, with impunity. The sessions were run by the local communist cadres, so no criticism of the Party or the Chinese was permitted, and thamzing simply became another method of attacking Tibetan values and Tibetan culture. Attendance was compulsory, inevitably.

The worst thing about thamzing was that the 'self-criticism' was not confined to words alone. 'Reactionaries' could expect a sound beating, and anyone who did not join in the general denunciation and violence could expect to be one of the next victims. There are still many people who are crippled, or deaf, or partially or completely blinded, as a result of beatings received during thamzing sessions.

Those who escaped beatings in thamzing might still not be safe from assault. The Chinese government policy favours birth control – to the extent of compulsory sterilisation. Given the pressures of the over-population in China, this is perhaps not surprising, no matter how barbarous it may seem. But Tibet is not China: it is a huge country, and thinly populated. The only reason for compulsory sterilisation there was to reduce the Tibetan population. Both men and women were sterilised, often with more enthusiasm than skill; one of the

The mystical and holy city of Lhasa has become a faceless metropolis; but in the old quarters, Tibet still survives as something more than a motif in the architecture.

delegations encountered a woman who was left paralysed below the waist, and incontinent, as the result of a Chinese 'sterilisation' operation. Once again, the scope for and the extent of abuse was immense.

There were other measures to try and wipe out the Tibetan race and culture, too. In the 1960s, compulsory marriages between Chinese and Tibetans were common. It is fair to argue that this must often have been as hard on the Chinese as on the Tibetans, but this does not begin to excuse the policy – or to remove the objection that it was being used to try to destroy Tibetan identity. Most of these marriages have since been annulled, and there were no new ones for some years, but in the mid-1980s a subtler policy was announced: the Chinese 'advisers' and 'technicians' who were sent to Tibet were all young men, and they were promised special privileges and better pay if they married Tibetan girls and settled in Tibet. Still more cynically, in order to attract the co-operation of Tibetan girls, the Chinese authorities have promised special treatment for the entire family of any Tibetan girl who married a Chinese. Although far less harsh than their earlier approach, this shows that the Chinese have still not altered their basic policy of trying to destroy Tibet as a nation and as a distinct culture.

Mass immigration from China has long been a way in which the Chinese sought to obliterate Tibet – and Chinese settlers are always allocated the choicest land, in Kongpo, Kham, and Amdo. Once again, it must be almost as hard for some of the compulsorily resettled Chinese as for the Tibetans, but at least the Tibetans had some chance of being able to cultivate their own land, based on experience: farming at high altitudes is not like low plains farming. The hardy Tibetan barley is the most practical crop over most of the plateau, but the Chinese do not like barley; the northern Chinese, from whom most of the settlers were drawn, are great wheat eaters. Furthermore

I did not realise until I saw this picture that there are lakes in Tibet which can float good-sized boats. There was never much of a fishing industry in old Tibet; indeed, 'eater of fish and chicken' was an insult.

the Chinese were often under the direction of a political officer who would order the planting of a totally unsuitable crop, which had no chance of growing, because it was 'in line with Mao Tse-Tung thought'. In time, the Chinese learned; meanwhile, the result was widespread famine and starvation, with the Chinese getting what little food there was.

The 1960s and early 1970s were, without doubt, the worst years of the Chinese occupation. They were also the years in which Tibetan resistance flourished. Tibetan guerrillas based in Mustang on the Nepalese/Tibetan border raided Chinese bases repeatedly, with the support of the CIA. Many guerrillas were drawn from the ranks of the erstwhile freedom fighters inside Tibet, and most had lost everything to the Chinese. They fought like men who had no other purpose.

There are innumerable stories of their exploits, though many are not told in public for fear that people still in Tibet will be recognised. One man who spent more than a year in the mountains with his parents tells how, as a child, he frequently saw men shot in front of him; on more than one occasion, a surprise Chinese attack meant that they lost everything except the clothes they stood up in, and their weapons; even their tsampa bowls would be left behind in the rush. Both he and his parents reached India.

Another, who fought with the Mustang guerrillas, recalls how the lack of medical facilities made toothache a real problem. For rapid energy they used to eat a lot of sugar which soon took its toll on their teeth. He tells of the leader of one band who handed a pair of pliers to his second-in-command and told him to pull out a painful tooth. The second-in-command protested that he could not do it; he had no idea of what to do, and would probably do more harm than good. The leader pulled his gun: "If you don't pull out my tooth, I'll blow your head off." The second-in-command pulled it, making a terrible mess in the process. The leader thanked him as best he could with a mouthful of blood, and as they rode along, he was actually laughing because the pain of the extraction was so much less than the pain of the tooth had been. Another man was less successful; he used battery acid to try to dissolve out an aching tooth, and had to be restrained from shooting himself because of the pain.

The American government apparently only ever regarded their involvement in Tibet as having nuisance value, although some of the CIA agents who fought with the Tibetans became devoted supporters of the Tibetan cause and even (in many cases) somewhat unorthodox Buddhists. As the era of Nixon's

A Khamba guerrilla with a gau, *or portable shrine containing a photograph of His Holiness, worn as an amulet.*

With 'liberalisation' came a modicum of restoration – but the people who do this work are, with few exceptions, doing it for nothing in their own time after working long and onerous hours for the Chinese.

rapprochement with the Chinese dawned, support for the armed resistance movement in Tibet was gravely reduced, and tailed off to nothing. Now the Americans sell helicopter gunships to the Chinese, and are talking about transferring nuclear technology.

The end of the 1970s marked a relaxation in the Chinese reign of terror in Tibet, but it is important to realise that this is true only in strictly relative terms. For example, pilgrimages are no longer banned in theory, but pilgrims lose their right to food rations for the duration of the pilgrimage, and might well be subjected to thamzing on their return if they belong to an old-fashioned commune.

On the subject of food, the basic ration in a typical commune in the 1970s was 12.5 *khels*, or about 175 kg, of grain per person per year. This works out to rather under half a kilo per day – about 1 lb. But grain was also the principal medium of barter for other foodstuffs, such as butter, salt, and (if you were lucky) a little meat, so a more realistic assessment of the amount of grain available might be 12 oz per person per day. It is true that 12 oz of tsampa goes a long way, but 4 oz (say 225 gm) per meal, with very little else, is approaching starvation level. Of course, no one starves under communism, so if someone died from lack of food (and it happened frequently), anyone who drew attention to the fact was branded as a 'rumour-monger and enemy of socialism'. In the schools, there were separate kitchens for Chinese and Tibetan children; the Tibetan children would forage in the waste-bins of the Chinese children's kitchen.

The list of stories which could be told is endless. Some are so petty that they would be funny in any other context. For example, there is an old tradition of singing satirical songs in the streets of Lhasa, a sort of Tibetan version of a West Indian calypso; when the Chinese found that they were the butt of some of these songs, they simply banned all singing in the streets. Another story, which well illustrates the deep cynicism and unpleasantness of the Chinese regime, concerns the 'Campaign to Eliminate Unnecessary Mouths'. This forced people to kill animals and bring them to the Chinese. A bizarre tariff was set up: so many flies equalled one mouse, so many mice were the equivalent to one cat or dog, and so forth. This is repulsive enough to anyone, but to a Tibetan Buddhist with an inbred regard for the sanctity of all life, it was agonising.

Understandably, all Chinese 'reforms' are regarded with deep suspicion by the Tibetans, and they are never quite what

Traditional Tibetan medicine is once again being encouraged – but many of the pills are for export only (to the Party leadership), and many traditionally trained Tibetans are in any case afraid to reveal their knowledge in case it leads to their being labelled 'reactionaries' in the next round of repression.

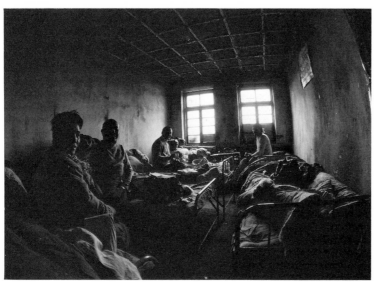

Typical living conditions for Tibetans in their own country are no better (and often worse) than for refugees in India.

The most precious thing that you can give to any Tibetan: a photograph of the Dalai Lama. Under Chinese customs regulations, only one picture per person is allowed into the country. This is of course a very old portrait, but it is one which is still popular with Tibetans both inside and outside Tibet.

they seem. The loss of food rations on pilgrimages, as quoted above, is just one example; another is the way in which people are now granted permission to leave Tibet in order to visit relatives – but must leave a close family member inside Tibet as a hostage against their return, and guarantee of their behaviour while they are away. Anything can be reversed at a moment's notice: the 'Let A Hundred Flowers Bloom' campaign was short lived, and those who dared to speak their minds 'disappeared' when it ended. Similarly, on his visit in 1980 Hu Yaobang promised that 85 per cent of Chinese civilian staff would be withdrawn from Tibet. A few were withdrawn – but more military personnel were drafted in, and then came tens of thousands of Chinese 'advisers' and 'technicians', who were to 'help in the development of Tibet'.

The high point of 'liberalisation' was probably 1982; since then, things have begun to deteriorate again. For example, in late 1983 about 2,500 'criminals' were arrested in Tibet. Some received the bullet in the back of the neck (the approved Chinese form of execution) almost immediately; some are known to be in labour camps; and some have simply 'disappeared'. For window-dressing, one Chinese was shot in the late 1983 executions: he was a common criminal who was executed with the Tibetan 'criminals', who were of course political dissidents. There is certainly hope for Tibet, in that things have improved since the 1960s, but the real hope in the hearts of all Tibetans inside and outside Tibet is that one day their country shall be free again, and ruled by His Holiness the Dalai Lama.

The policy of 'equality' in China and Chinese-occupied countries is not always followed, despite the avowals of the leadership. Here, Mrs Pema Gyalpo is received by a high Chinese official.

A WORLD IN EXILE

A culture is an intricate living web of customs, beliefs, rituals, tools, history, and necessity. The culture of the old Tibet, based though it was on the teachings of the Lord Buddha, was flawed: as the Dalai Lama himself said, "You have to admit that our religion needed purifying. For that, at least, we can be grateful to the Chinese."

The flaws, in the view of His Holiness, were an unwillingness to face the necessity for change in a modern world; an excessive regard for the forms and ritual of religion, as opposed to its purpose; and too great a readiness to rely on others, rather than on oneself. His own position showed this last fault all too clearly: in Tibet and in exile, his attempts to make people more self-reliant and less dependent upon him have met with limited success.

It was these flaws which enabled the Chinese to invade and occupy Tibet. Had Tibet been a member of the United Nations; had there been a modern army, strengthened (as the Great Thirteenth had wished) by men drafted out of monasteries which they only occupied from force of habit; had the leaders of the great monasteries not blocked the reforms suggested by the Great Thirteenth, with the full support of the people; then, Tibet might still be free.

The Chinese have tried to destroy Tibetan culture, perhaps inevitably, since it was based upon religion. They have failed, and they will continue to fail, just as the Russians have failed to wipe out Christianity, Islam, and Buddhism within the borders of their empire: in a state where the material comforts of life are so conspicuously lacking, spiritual comforts are all the more necessary. In this sense, they have failed to conquer Tibet. They have, however, managed to destroy many of the manifestations of religion, as well as many other aspects of the culture. This places a unique responsibility on the Tibetans in exile.

For the sake of history and scholarship, if nothing else, they must preserve what they can salvage: if whole traditions

of art, of sculpture, of music, of Buddhist learning were to disappear without trace, the loss to humanity would be incalculable. Far more than this, they must also preserve the skills which are needed to ensure the continuation of these traditions if they are to preserve their own culture. The ornate wood-carvings which decorate the temples; the religious statues, in clay and metal; the *thangka* paintings; thefolk operas, drama and dance; the intricate religious chants; the transmission of the various schools of Buddhism; all of these require *people* if the Tibetan culture is not to disappear into museums and libraries. And they require people *now*: a skill that is lost can be lost forever.

There would be little point, however, in trying to preserve Tibetan culture unchanged. Such an attempt would be doomed in any case: the impact of the West, even filtered through India, cannot be ignored. It would be a waste of time, since it would propagate precisely those faults which led to Tibet's downfall in the first place. What is needed, therefore, is a reconstruction of Tibetan culture, preserving all that is

Images of the old Tibet still remain even in exile: these young novices play in the courtyard of their monastery as their teachers played – only their teachers played in Tibet, and they play in southern India.

The new Tibet: at Bylakuppe, in southern India, Tibetans make subcontracted parts for Indian industry, and in Sikkim there is an embryonic Tibetan watch manufacturing industry.

New Year's morning: prostrations at the temple, before the dawn ceremonies start.

good, and adding to it what is necessary to ensure survival in the modern world.

This massive task has been made easier by a number of factors. The most important is the Dalai Lama himself. Not only does he work tirelessly for his people; they, in turn, are prepared to follow him almost without question. Many have gathered themselves around him, settling in Dharamsala, and others have been willing to go to the various settlements in India, as he directs.

Secondly, the Tibetan people have received a great deal of help from the outside world. India must head the list, for the extraordinary generosity with which land, money, and materials have been made available to the Tibetans, but there have been many other donors great and small. Innumerable refugee organisations and individuals have given time and money to the Tibetans in exile. For example, the various children's houses at the Tibetan Children's Village in Dharamsala, which looks after Tibetan orphans and semi-orphans, each bear the name of the donors. The list is impressive: Dutch Aid to Tibetans, Norwegian Aid to Tibetans, the Gmeiner Foundation from Germany, Swedish charities set up especially to help Tibetans. Again, among the Tibetan teachers at the Village (which is universally known as TCV), there have always been a few non-Tibetan teachers – English, American, Australian, and even Japanese – as well as a few Indians, and at the Delek Hospital there are several non-Tibetan doctors and nurses, as well as a Tibetan doctor trained in Western medicine. They work for board and pocket money, doing what they can.

The third factor is the character of the Tibetan people. Fiercely proud of being Tibetan, they are determined to preserve their religion and their culture, come what may. This national pride is not just confined to the old people: young Tibetans, even in Switzerland and Canada, are equally conscious of their roots. There was a period in the late 1960s and early 1970s when it looked as if Tibetans born outside Tibet were losing their culture, and becoming completely westernised, but this seems now to have been merely a question of reaction: they have learned what they want from the West, and what they want from their own culture, and have successfully integrated the two. On the other hand, Tibetans in exile have also proved themselves extremely adaptable. Time and again, Westerners are astonished by the way in which cultural differences between themselves and Tibetans are far less than they expected – so small, in fact, that it is often possible to forget that there are any. This is all the more striking in Dharamsala, where the comparison with India is all too clear, but perhaps it is most remarkable in Switzerland. There, the Tibetans are concentrated just outside Zurich; the contrast between the friendly, easy-going Tibetans and the reserved, not to say dour, Zurichers is quite spectacular, despite the fact that one would expect visitors to have far more in common with the citizens of a modern European democracy than with the products of a feudal oriental theocracy.

Self-sufficiency is the rule everywhere: little workshops (the Chinese would call them 'factories') turn out carpets, clothes, or (as here) traditional felt shoes.

Opposite *His Holiness the Dalai Lama, the Great Seal of Tibet in front of him, speaks at the 25th anniversary of the National Uprising which took place in 1959.*

Above left *Among the crowd this refugee carries an English language placard expressing the determination of the Tibetan people.*

Right and above right *The Dalai Lama's audience, young and old, lay and monk, listens intently; in the old Tibet, protocol would have prevented them from ever hearing the voice of the Inmost One.*

In an unofficial ending to the 25th anniversary commemoration, small boys (well primed with tea) urinate on the Chinese flag and an effigy of Teng-shou-ping (Deng Xiaoping).

Generalisations are well known to be dangerous, however, and the Tibetans demonstrate this very well. There is no such thing as the 'Tibetan character', because Tibet (like any nation) is made up of individuals. For example, the Dalai Lama has a younger brother called Tendzin Choegyal. TC, as he is known to his friends, is the eighth in line of incarnate lamas who bear the name Ngari Rinpoche; but he cheerfully says that there is no way he could have been Tibetan in previous incarnations. Instead, he says, he is a Westerner who merely happened to be reborn as a Tibetan. "I'm a banana," he says, "yellow on the outside and white on the inside." But regardless of what he says (and it is often impossible to tell when he or any of his brothers or his sisters are joking), he works long hours in the Private Office of the Dalai Lama for next to no salary, and many who have been fortunate enough to have long conversations with him are convinced that he is actually one of the best teachers that they have encountered.

Examples could be multiplied indefinitely. Jamyang Norbu, the Director of the Tibetan Institute for Performing Arts, was educated at a Jesuit school in India, regards English rather than Tibetan as his primary language, and is one of the strongest critics of the Administration in Exile. But he continues to run the Institute, receiving in return only board (in a two-roomed hut with a shared outside toilet) and a minute salary, because "If I don't do it, who will?". He earns a little money on the side from short story writing, and could return to the journalism at which he once made a living; but he does not. The Editor of the *Tibetan Review*, Tsering Wangyal, was educated at Bristol University and has (in the finest journalistic tradition) a weakness for good Scotch; but he lives in one room in Delhi, producing the magazine every month almost single-handed, and has to console his palate with Binnie's Aristocrat Genuine Malt Whisky, made in India. Few Englishmen could equal his command of the English language.

Lobsang Samten, another of the Dalai Lama's brothers, runs the Tibetan Medical Institute, a combination of hospital, pharmacy, and medical school for traditional Tibetan medicine. His sister, Mrs Pema Gyalpo, runs the Tibetan Children's Village. Of the Gyari family, an ancient clan from Kham, one is joint head of the Information Office of the Dalai Lama in Dharamsala, and another heads the Office of His Holiness in Tokyo; another sister and brother work in the travel business, but also make their talents available to the Administration.

How does a pacifist and a vegetarian make a tiger-skin rug? Tibetan weavers in Kalimpong have solved the problem. The dragon design is traditional, the tiger is novel, and the city scene is a fascinating piece of modern art.

Again in Kalimpong, a mask-maker carves masks based on traditional Lhamo *and* Cham *patterns for the tourist trade. Few people object; it is more important that he earns a living than that the masks are kept secret.*

Spinning and weaving are another way of earning money. Some sales will be to Tibetans and Nepalese; others to Indians; and yet others to tourists.

In Bir, one of the few Tibetan colonies not intimately linked with Dharamsala, a woman in a traditional hat carries animal fodder. She wears a traditional tengwar *or 108-bead rosary around her neck.*

With such a pool of willing talent, the Dalai Lama is able to lead what amounts to a Government-in-Exile in India, though the term 'Administration' is normally used to show that there is no usurpation of Indian jurisdiction. The minute salaries which it pays come partly from donations given by Tibetans in India, partly from money given by Tibetans living abroad, and partly from funds raised by the Dalai Lama himself and his Economic Affairs Office (the Paljor Office). The trouble is that although in almost all of the senior posts, and in many of the junior ones, are idealists working for love rather than for money, the tiny salaries are insufficient to attract the right people to fill the remaining jobs. This, combined with a certain predilection for empire-building among the heads of the various departments, means that things do not always run as smoothly as they might. The Administration in Exile is probably no less efficient than any other government, and a good deal more efficient than some, but the very small scale on which it operates means that any problems are there for all to see; they cannot be covered up, as they are in most bigger governments.

It would, however, be foolish as well as churlish to dwell upon the shortcomings of the Administration, because they are trivial next to its accomplishments. It has helped something over a hundred thousand refugees to find a place to live, and a means of livelihood; it has supported old crafts, and encouraged new ones; it has organised schools, and sent many students on to higher education; it has preserved many aspects of Tibetan culture, from religion to the arts; and it has kept the Tibetan question alive. It also provides the support for the Dalai Lama's travels, for he has become a leader of world significance, comparable in many ways to His Holiness the Pope. It is worth considering these accomplishments in order.

The earliest refugees, between 1950 and 1959, tended to concentrate around Kalimpong and Darjeeling. These were traditional centres of trade between Tibet and India, and there had always been a strong Tibetan presence there. When His Holiness came out, in 1959, most refugees wanted to be near him; Mussoorie, the hill station above Dehra Dun where he was lent a cottage, became the focal point of the refugee community. At first, it seemed that there might be some possibility of returning to Tibet, but after a few months it became obvious that the exile would be prolonged. The Indian government, in association with the Dalai Lama's advisers, drew up a short list of suitable places for a Tibetan colony. Dharamsala, about three hundred miles north-east of Delhi, was the site finally chosen.

An old woman spinning wool: a timeless image. In normal times, this old woman would be the matriarch of a family. But instead of telling stories to her grandchilden, she is a refugee who fled the Chinese invaders when she was already well into middle age, and now lives in the old people's section of the Tibetan Children's Village.

As soon as you get off the bus in McLeod Ganj, you are besieged with a bewildering array of signposts. This picture was taken in March 1982.

'Dharamsala' is actually a number of settlements on the Dhauladur spur of the Himalayas, ranging in height from 4,000 feet to over 6,000 feet. The lower settlements, Lower Dharamsala and Kotwali Bazaar (a *kotwali* is a police station), are predominantly Indian, but the higher settlements are Tibetan. McLeod Ganj is the biggest, and the most completely Tibetan, of these.

Even now, it is not much to look at. At the top of the town there is a sort of square where the buses stop, more a confluence of roads than a planned open space. There is the main road up from Dharamsala, up which the bus grinds for two thousand feet vertically and about seven miles horizontally along a series of hairpin bends and through Forsyth Ganj, past the Church of St John in the Wilderness, which was built in the days when Dharamsala was a fashionable hill station for the Raj; the sometime Viceroy, Lord Elgin, is buried there. Clockwise from there, two roads lead by slightly different routes to Forsyth Bazaar (the Scottish influence was strong), above which the Tibetan Children's Village now is situated. TCV is about a mile or a mile and a half from McLeod Ganj, and one or two hundred feet higher. Clockwise again, there are two more roads, one leading up to the Drama School (or the Tibetan Institute for Performing Arts, as it is officially known), and one winding around to Bhagsunath village, two or three miles away and a little lower than McLeod Ganj, passing as it does so both a Government of India seismological survey station and the monastery of Ngakpa Rinpoche.

On the opposite side of the square from where the buses come in, there are the two main streets of McLeod Ganj. They are rough and broken, with exposed water pipes and open gutters, which can smell quite strong in hot weather. The more important of the two streets houses most of the shops; the other has the fronts of shops along one side, but the backs of the shops in the other street along the other. These two roads are perhaps sixty or seventy yards long. Down beside one of them runs one of the many paths which the visitor to Dharamsala keeps discovering. This one used to be motorable, but it is no longer possible to take even a jeep very far down it now; subsidence, minor landslips, and rocks that have fallen on to the road mean that a trail motorcycle is the only powered vehicle which could negotiate it. Dharamsala is in earthquake country, though the last big earthquake was in 1905. That was what ended its pre-eminence as a hill station, and crazily split and sloping paths still bear witness to what it must have been like. At the far end of the two main roads –

from the square, that is – there are two more roads and a drive. The drive leads up to the Bhagsu Hotel, owned by the Himachal Pradesh Tourist Corporation, whilst the left-hand road leads down to Kotwali Bazaar by a much more precipitous route than the buses take: it rises the same distance, obviously, but in rather under three miles, so that it is as quick to walk up from Kotwali Bazaar as to take the bus. This road passes the Delek Hospital (western style) and the Tibetan Medical Institute (Tibetan medicine), as well as Gangchen Kyishong, where many of the offices of the Government in Exile are situated. At Gangchen Kyishong too are the Library of Tibetan works and Archives (LTWA), and Nechung and Gathong Monastery, home of the State Oracle of Tibet. The other road, which ultimately joins this one rather above Gangchen Kyishong, passes Thekchen Choeling, the 'Great-Path Dharma-Place' or Place of Mahayana. This comprises some more offices of the Administration, the monastery of Phendey Lekshey Ling (of which, since it was founded, there have always been 175 members including the Dalai Lama), the Temple, and the residence, office, and audience rooms of His Holiness the Dalai Lama.

All this is a far cry from the Lhasa plain, with the great Potala dominating the scene, and the crag of the Chakpori medical school in the background, but it is widely known as Little Lhasa. Wherever the Dalai Lama is, there is the centre of Tibet. Each year, the visitor can see a few more improvements: more new buildings, such as the magnificent new Nechung monastery which was completed in 1984, more reliable supplies of water and electricity (when the previous transformer burned out, in 1982, McLeod Ganj was without electricity for ten days), more goods in the shops, better dressed people, more choice of food in the restaurants (though this also depends to a great extent on the seasons), more events such as film-shows, slide-shows and dramatic performances, and so forth. To anyone unfamiliar with India, it is still squalid, crowded, poor, and malodorous; but next to most Indian villages, it is a model of prosperity. Indeed, it is sometimes hard to remember that you are in a refugee colony, and sometimes very hard indeed to remember that you are in India.

The best place to begin a description of McLeod Ganj is where most people start: at the bus stop, opposite Nowrojee's Store, founded 1862. Mr Nowrojee, an elderly Parsee, presides over the biggest shop in Dharamsala, and the only liquor store in McLeod Ganj (which ensures a steady stream of Tibetan custom), but it is obvious that the shop has seen better days. The dark, dusty shop is as much a museum as shop; some of

Again in March, a year later, the weather is a lot warmer and the deep porch of Nowrojee's Store (Established 1860) provides shade which grows ever more welcome as the weather heats up.

the goods on display are not for sale, such as the Edwardian mourning stationery, many of the signs would fetch a fortune in Western antique shops, and even the goods that are for sale are displayed in incredibly venerable cabinets and bottles. The Amul chocolate bars, for example, dwell in an enormously tall cylindrical glass bottle with an elegantly shaped top. The main concession to modernity is the drinks cooler, from which Mr Nowrojee dispenses lemonade, cola, and soda-water of his own bottling. He is justly proud of these, for they are considerably better than the ubiquitous Thums Up (sic), Campa Cola, and Limca.

Few Tibetans shop there, except for the liquor. The Tibetan shops, which line the main street, are much smaller, more crowded, and livelier. Some sell genuine Tibetan antiquities; many more sell fakes or (to be charitable, or if the buyer is not gullible) modern replicas, in varying qualities. Some of the handicrafts, mainly brass and jewellery, are made in Nepal, but there are also plenty of genuinely Tibetan goods on sale. There are shops that sell clothes, whether Tibetan shirts and *chubas* or Western (or imitation Western) jeans and jackets.

105

Others sell cloth, though the best fabric shops are in Kotwali Bazaar, and among the grocery and hardware shops selling matches, candles, plastic jugs and buckets, flip-flops and the like, you can buy specifically Tibetan requirements: brick tea, for making the salted butter-tea which is the traditional Tibetan drink, or *katags*, the ceremonial white scarves which are presented as a mark of respect, or between friends at meetings or partings, or lengths of brightly-coloured cord like technicolour bootlaces, which lamas tie into 'protection cords' for anyone who asks.

The food shops are not impressive; in fact, the meat and fish shops are enough to turn the stomach of most Westerners. It is best either to be a vegetarian, or not to think too hard about the antecedents of your meal. The vegetable shops are rather better, though prices are (relatively) high because of the transport costs. Very little food is grown in the mountains, and most of it is trucked in from the plains. There are periodical shortages of things, as the bus which was carrying that particular consignment goes off the road.

Inevitably, because it is essentially a Tibetan village, there is a big *chorten* or religious monument in the middle of the centre block of shops. The literal meaning of 'chorten' is 'receptacle of mind', and the chorten itself is symbolic on many levels of the Mind of the Buddha; among its other symbols, it indicates universality by incorporating the symbols of Earth, Water,

A typical small store in Dharamsala, selling pulses, grain, and a few vegetables.

Traders who cannot even afford awnings and regular pitches set up their stalls around the central stupa in the main street.

Just below the stupa is a tiny temple with a huge prayer wheel, which can just be seen through the door in this picture.

Fire, Air, and Space. It is flanked on both sides by rows of prayer wheels, and there is also a tiny temple with a huge prayer wheel in it. Each time the wheel revolves, it strikes a little bell, so that the rhythmic ting...ting...ting...ting of the prayer wheel is a regular background to the other noises of Dharamsala.

The main temple, though, is over at Thekchen Choeling, the main religious complex. At first sight to a Western eye, it is curiously evocative of a classical Greek temple, especially to one accustomed to the exuberance of colour and wood-carving which characterises so many other Tibetan temples. Inside, it is much more colourful. The great throne, draped in the Five Auspicious Colours (red, green, yellow, blue, and white) is one of the focal points; when His Holiness is on it, it is *the* focal point. There are statues, too: Tsong Khapa, the Great Reformer of Tibetan Buddhism and founder of the Gelugpa school (of which His Holiness is a member), the Lord Buddha himself, Avolokiteshvara, the Buddha of Compassion, and a particularly impressive representation of Guru Rinpoche (Padmasambhava, the Lotus Born), who brought Buddhism to the common people of Tibet in AD 747. On high days and holy days, the interior of the temple will be packed, and those who cannot get seats inside (which means most, for it would be hard pressed to hold six hundred people) spill outside, onto the surrounding path and the lawn in front. At

On either side of the stupa are large fixed prayer wheels; people give them a spin as they pass, the more devout taking care to go clockwise as they do so.

Monlam, the great prayer festival just after Losar (New Year), there will be a thousand or more people on the lawn, listening to His Holiness's teaching. Before the teachings, they will circumambulate the temple (always clockwise; the followers of the ancient Bon religion go anticlockwise around their temples), each spinning the big, heavy prayer-wheels set along the back and side of the temple.

The tourist will probably stay at the Hotel Bhagsu, or the Hotel Tibet; those who are less affluent will check into one of the cheaper hotels, such as the Green Hotel, whilst those who are both in the know and well off will first check Kashmir Cottage, where the Dalai Lama's sister-in-law sometimes takes paying guests; she and her husband Tendzin Choegyal, who works in the Private Office of His Holiness, both say that they would like to derive enough income from this so that they can cease drawing his salary and save the Administration money. Their house is as comfortable as most in the west (though rather cold in winter), and there are a few others who enjoy similar standards, but for the most part, even quite well-off Tibetans live in conditions which seem rather primitive and cramped by Western standards. Two rooms, or at most three, with a kitchen and bathoom are all that most Tibetan refugees aspire to, and this is luxury.

Most people live in single rooms with a couple of cots where

The main temple at Thekchen Choeling, with the Dhauladur mountain range looming behind it.

The river Bhagsu, about four miles from McLeod Ganj, is the only place where laundry can be done in comfort, and a bath enjoyed with a (very small) measure of privacy.

Come the spring, it is warm enough to wash the children in the streets again – even if the children do not always think so.

a carpet is the only mattress between them and the wood. In the daytime, these cots or benches are cleared (except for the carpet) and used as seats; at night, they are the beds. A pressure-stove at the other end of the room provides the kitchen; water comes from a shared tap, which may be a hundred yards or more away. Some use the shared toilets, built in blocks, which can be equally far away; others prefer to use a quiet spot a few yards from the road, or behind the houses. A drawback of one favoured spot is that it is used by monkeys for the same purpose, and they can sometimes be rather possessive about territory. A bath may be a rarity for adults – a dip in the river Bhagsu, three miles away – though children are washed rather more frequently. It is not that Tibetans are dirty people by choice, as is shown by their enthusiasm for showers when they have the chance: it is just the lack of opportunity. This was still more true in the old Tibet, because of the cold, though there were thermal springs in some areas that were well patronised.

What is remarkable is how un-squalid most of these tiny shacks, or single rooms in larger buildings, actually are. The mountain air has something to do with it, but the main factor is something far more important: the love, openness, and friendliness of even the poorest Tibetans. What they have, they share. They do not just share it with their old friends:

109

Above right *Inside Ama-la's house (Ama-la means 'respected mother', and is the standard term of respect to an older woman who is a close friend or relative, whether she is anyone's mother or not). She lives with her family in one room, of which approximately half is shown here.*

Above left *Water has to be fetched from a shared and unreliable tap. Ama-la is lucky: the tap is just outside her door. This lady lives a few yards away, but some have to walk three or four hundred yards.*

Right *The shrine in Ama-la's house. The sprouting barley is a part of the New Year offerings; another item on the shrine is a home-made prayer wheel adapted from a jam jar.*

Opposite *Refugee homes in Dharamsala follow the Tibetan pattern: children play alongside precipitous drops, and never seem to get hurt. The only real clues which show that this picture was taken in the 1980s in Dharamsala instead of twenty or even fifty years earlier in Tibet are the galvanised roof and the watch that Pema Yangtzom is wearing.*

they share it with new-found friends (though some are very diffident about allowing Western friends to see the sort of place they live in), and they share it with all sentient beings through the teachings of the Lord Buddha. Some things bring home the meaning of poverty: a home-made prayer-wheel inside a jam-jar, with the spindle protruding through a hole punched in the lid, where it can be spun by the family or by visitors. A shrine lit with one of those flickering candle-effect lamps, and decorated with a Western Christmas-tree ornament. The immediate Western reaction may be to wince at the taste; but when you have *nothing*, you make do with what you can. It is said that in the Potala there were offering mandalas made up of precious stones in vessels of gold; but a handful of

Above *On the roof of the temple: the Losar (New Year) ceremonies, presided over by His Holiness the Dalai Lama, begin before dawn and go on for several hours.*

Butter-tormas, ritual 'cakes' made entirely from coloured butter, are displayed in the temple during the Losar ceremonies.

Tea is an integral part of all Tibetan life, and religious rituals are no exception. Each monk carries his own tea-bowl with him wherever he goes.

rice in a chipped bowl is as precious, because the offering itself is not in the world of illusion where there are diamonds, gold, and rice, but in the heart.

To speak of the dignity of poverty is nonsense, unless perhaps you have taken some sort of vow – ask anyone who has been poor. But these people show that poverty cannot destroy dignity. The guest is offered tea or *chang* (barley beer), *khabse* (home-made fried biscuits), perhaps dried meat or even an egg. His hosts are aware they are very poor; and they are also aware that they are free.

Little Lhasa is unlike other Tibetan settlements in India in that there is no agriculture to speak of. The inhabitants derive their income from working for the Administration in various ways, from hotel-keeping and shopkeeping, and from handicrafts. There are also several monasteries, and branches of monasteries, but (as in Tibet) these survive mainly on contributions from outside.

As is already clear, there are many opportunities for government service. The funding of the various bodies varies enormously: for example, the Library of Tibetan Works and Archives is supported by the Indian government, as befits one of the most important libraries in its field. Other offices, such as the Information Office, are funded almost entirely by the Administration, though some income derives from the sale of books (including this one) and souvenirs such as car stickers, T-shirts, and badges with messages about Tibet. Several Tibetan offices issue T-shirts; the best probably come from the Institute of Performing Arts. This may seem an odd sideline for a government in Exile, but they are very effective at broadcasting the Tibetan message.

Mani *stones carved with* mantras, *are often bought by pilgrims to add to cairns. Sometimes, boulders will be carved and painted in* situ, *as here at Tso.Pema.*

The Nyingma monastery at Tso.Pema gleams in its surroundings as Tibetan monasteries used to gleam: it is all too easy to forget that the pictures we see of modern Tibet show the results of decades of neglect, and usually of wanton destruction as well.

The whole spirit of the Administration is informal, and surprisingly young. Collars and ties are virtually unheard of, and most men wear open-necked shirts and trousers of Western design, only wearing Tibetan dress for formal occasions such as religious ceremonies at the temple, National Uprising Day, and so forth. Traditional dress is more common among women, partly due to some rather old-fashioned attitudes on the part of older people, but mostly because it is a rare combination of practicality and femininity. It is far from universal, however.

Although the Tibetan Children's Village is actually separate from the Administration proper, being funded entirely by its own trusts and donations (the Indian government no longer contributes, though it did in the crucial early days and for many years after that), as well as by sponsorship of individual children, it does illustrate very well how a typical office works. At its head is Mrs Pema Gyalpo, His Holiness's younger sister. Some have criticised her as autocratic, or found her hard to get on with, but this is hardly fair. She is strong willed, it is true, but she has to be in order to run a school that is literally the size of a village, with over twelve hundred residential pupils and perhaps another hundred who attend on a daily basis. She is also responsible for schools in other Tibetan settlements, with between two and three thousand more children! She is, however, a very private person, who likes to keep her job and her personal life entirely separate, not in the sense that she walks

Those who cannot get into the temple during the Losar ceremonies crowd around outside. Most will stay for the entire cycle of rituals, which begins before dawn (they will arrive at six or six-thirty) and ends well after ten o'clock in the morning.

Below *These* Cham *dances are being held in the courtyard of the Nyingma monastery at Tso.Pema. A young acolyte holds the* dung-chen *(great horns) which his seniors play. Each blows in turn, taking over from the other, so the deep unearthly sound can continue for minutes on end. It can be heard over great distances.*

out of her office and ceases to think about her schools, but in the sense that anyone who has official business with her must approach through the proper channels, while her private life is her own in the same way as anyone else's. By the same token, she does not take kindly to people who press her about her relationship with the Dalai Lama, and she has been known to be rather short with Westerners who adopt Tibetan names and clothes without going any deeper (and there are plenty of those in Dharamsala), but she loaned several negatives from her private collection in order to have prints made for this book. She is five or six years younger than the Dalai Lama.

Her staff are almost all younger than she is: the Headmaster

Tibetans place great store by education, and children are usually educated to be at least trilingual (Tibetan, Hindi and English) and often quadrilingual, if the local language is not Hindi – and each language uses a different alphabet! This is a village school in Chhauntra.

116

of the Senior School – a title to strike fear into the heart of any errant child – is in his thirties, and sits in his big, bare office dressed in denim. Not expensive, new, beautifully-cut denim, but comfortable, worn old jeans. Yet the children in the school have impeccable manners, with many of the courtesies which are all but forgotten in the West: standing up as an adult enters the room, calling male visitors 'sir', and so forth. Seeing them, one is acutely aware that education is a privilege, not a tiresome necessity.

A few of the teachers are temporary, working for a year or two or three, Western-trained and taking some time off between college and embarking on their regular careers, or taking time out from the step-ladder of promotion to do something that they feel is worthwhile. The material rewards are low: salaries are just pocket-money, accommodation is comfortable but scarcely luxurious, and there are many out-of-school duties, but the compensations are legion. The children want to learn; there is virtually no indiscipline; and there is a feeling of being wanted, of doing a useful job that is appreciated by the whole community, instead of being some sort of child-minder. The vast majority of the teachers are Tibetans, who have been trained either in India or in the West. Some are actually graduates of TCV, so the system is self-perpetuating. Almost all Tibetans, including His Holiness, are passionate believers in the value of education.

The facilities are very varied. The living accommodation for the senior boys and girls compares favourably with any school, anywhere, but the laboratories (for example) are very sparely furnished. They have some modern apparatus, but it is normally rather precious and is used for demonstrations by the teacher rather than for experiments by the pupils. Where materials and equipment are more reasonably priced, as in elementary chemistry, the pupils learn experimental technique. There is perhaps more emphasis on rote learning than in the West, including chanting in order to memorise facts, but this is typical of India. It is also a matter of fashion; many new techniques have been found less effective.

The age range of the pupils is considerable. There is a special 'baby home' which accepts even babies whose mothers have died in childbirth. There is a kindergarten, in which some of the teachers are monks: it is fascinating to see a child learning his (English) ABC beside a shaven-headed monk in full-skirted maroon robes, whilst another monk walks around the open-plan classroom checking the work of children who are assembling sentences from words pasted onto slips of

Severe overcrowding is the rule in this nursery for orphans near Darjeeling. There are tragically many Tibetan orphans and many 'semi-orphans' where one parent has died and the other is unable both to work and look after the child.

Opposite *Science is taught in English, while a monk teaches Tibetan in the classroom next door. In this school in Hunsur, the Headmistress is an anglophone Indian.*

Right *The recreational facilities at The Tibetan Children's Village in Dharamsala might be the envy of some Western schools. TCV is sufficiently well funded to be able to afford some very fine buildings.*

paper. There is a junior school, which is where most of the chanting learning goes on; these younger children live together in dormitories, on a sort of family basis. There are two dormitories, one for boys and one for girls, in each house-unit, and each dormitory holds ten to fourteen children. In some house-units there will be a house-mother and a house-father, but in others there will just be a house-mother. At least one house-mother is a nun, which rather precludes a house-father!

The senior school is separate, though on the same site as the rest of TCV, and as already mentioned the two-person study dormitories are impressive. There are posters on the wall, just as in any school, but the constant reappearance of pictures of the Dalai Lama is a powerful reminder that this is not a typical Western school. The boys' dormitories are about as far from the girls' as is realistically possible within the constraints of the site, so presumably some problems are constant throughout the world.

In addition to these obvious divisions, however, there is also a unit which provides a crash course for new refugees from Tibet; a vocational training school, for a number of handicrafts; and an old people's home. The new refugee unit is designed to teach basic English and Hindi for shopping, together with an introduction to life in India. In it, you will find children of seven or eight beside hulking youths of seventeen or eighteen, and a few in their twenties. Those who wish can also enter the regular school system, so that in some classes there will be one or two who are much older than the rest. The vocational training school teaches basic dressmaking and tailoring (Tibetan *couture* is hardly more subtle than Tibetan *cuisine*), together with carpet weaving, *thangka* painting, and some craft skills. There are other schools which are more highly regarded for certain skills, however: the leading thangka painting school is run by the Library of Tibetan Works and Archives, and so is the main wood-carving school, but there is another small wood-carving school alongside the metalwork school (which makes everything from ten-foot-high Buddhas to jewellery), just along from Kotwali Bazaar. The old people's home arose as a natural extension of the original TCV aim of looking after those who could not look after themselves. The old people are encouraged to do light work, such as spinning, and to pass on any traditional skills that they may have.

The kind of overlap already illustrated by the schools occurs in many other places. For example, there are a few elderly bedridden patients at the Tibetan Medical Institute, which is just down the road from Gangchen Kyishong, though the

121

main function of this institution is to keep Tibetan medicine alive. In addition to a hospital and pharmacy, the Medical Institute is also a medical school and a factory for traditional Tibetan medicines. Many Tibetans, especially the better educated ones, shuttle freely between Western and Tibetan medicine. There are some things that Western medicine cures quickly and far more effectively than Tibetan medicine, but there are also conditions (mostly chronic) which do not yield to Western medicine but which can successfully be treated with Tibetan medicines. There are some remedies, such as the *jaa* poultice for sprains, which seem to work better than anything else, and others such as Precious Purified Moon Crystals which sound as if they owe as much to magic as to science, but for which some users have reported truly magical results. The Tibetan Medical Institute also houses the School of Astrology, whose business it is to calculate auspicious timings for official events,but who will also prepare individual horoscopes on request, for a modest sum.

The Library or LTWA is a multi-faceted organisation. In addition to their obvious function as guardians of books both Tibetan and Western, the staff are responsible for the Tibetan Picture Library (from which some of the pictures in this book were taken), and for a museum of Tibetan art and artefacts which contains many items on loan from His Holiness. Even then, it is not exactly a museum in the sense that a Westerner would understand: the centrepiece is a magnificent carved

Opposite above left Under a picture of the Dalai Lama, Tibetan medicine is dispensed at the Tibetan Medical Institute and at its branch (seen here) in McLeod Ganj. Many Tibetan doctors are women, but as a rule, men prefer to be treated by male doctors.

Opposite above right A few very old and sick patients who have nowhere else to go are maintained at the main branch of the Tibetan Medical Institute. There is little that either Western or Tibetan medicine can do for them, but their last days can be made as comfortable as possible.

Opposite below The Tibetan pharmacopoeia is complex, but methodical; this is the main store-room for drugs and herbs at the Tibetan Medical Institute.

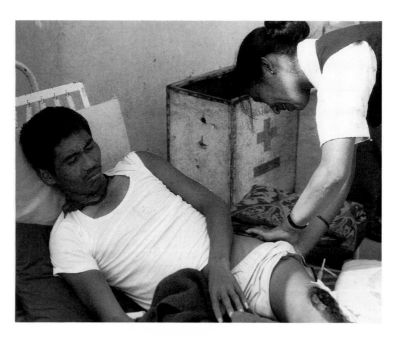

Western medicine is dispensed at the Delek Hospital in Dharamsala. This man is suffering from a bone abscess which has erupted through the leg; with antibiotic treatment, it should subside, but it will recur. Amputation is a possibility, but as the doctor said, "Maybe it's better to have a painful leg which erupts sometimes rather than no leg at all."

The Library of Tibetan Works and Archives maintains separate Tibetan and foreign-language reading rooms; the foreign-language room is usually well patronised.

Below *A rather less expected aspect of the LTWA is the fact that it runs both a* thangka-*painting school and a wood-carving school in an annexe.*

The thangka *painting school which is part of the Library of Tibetan Works and Archives.*

three-dimensional mandala, and most of one wall is taken up with a massive altar piece. Both were carved in Dharamsala in the 1970s and 1980s. The Library also organises courses on Buddhism, and even administers a few rooms for the use of visiting scholars – which may also be let out if there are no scholars.

Another body with the Administration which is responsible for preserving Tibetan culture is the TIPA, or Tibetan Institute for Performing Arts, which has already been mentioned briefly. This is responsible for the secular performing arts (the religious ones are kept alive in the monasteries), but it also manages to keep a sculptor on the premises, who is skilled in the manufacture of images of deities. The Institute normally runs a festival every year, in the second month of the Tibetan calendar (March or April), with *Lhamo* performances as well as more modern non-traditional works and the equivalent of children's pantomimes. Lhamo (folk-opera) performances are always well attended, though the ex-director of the Institute, Jamyang Norbu, likened them more to an English village cricket match than a Western play. They go on all day, with a break for lunch, and the audience may chat among themselves or picnic on food, tea, and chang that they have brought with them. Everyone knows the plots, so there is no danger of missing anything very much, but it makes a pleasant day out.

Left *The dramatic costumes of the Tibetan Institute of Performing Arts were all lost in a disastrous fire in 1984, and they were still trying to replace them at the time of writing (1985). This is the Hunter, whose role is the ritual purification of the stage.*

Opposite *Dancers from the Tibetan Institute of Performing Arts perform at various public ceremonies; this is at the Democracy Day celebrations in Dharamsala in September 1983.*

Below Lhamo, *or folk-opera, was performed regularly at the TIPA until the disastrous fire. This picture, taken in early 1984, shows the Ambassadors from the Land of Wisdom (India) in front of the Chinese Emperor's throne in the popular play* The Chinese Princess, *which tells the story of the Chinese princess given in marriage to the King of Tibet. The great awning, which was also lost in the fire, is known as the 'Inner Sky'.*

Those who do not work within the Administration in one way or another are often shopkeepers, and indeed some shops sell products from Administration-owned workshops. For a visitor, the most interesting shops are those which sell Tibetan antiques and neo-antiques. The truth is that Tibetan technology changed so little over the centuries that even experts have difficulty in dating anything much before 1950: the best that can be done is to assign a century, or 'early, mid, or late' inside that century. Tibetans judge things more by the quality of workmanship, and by the way in which they have been used, than by chronological age: a fine *dorje* and *drilbu* (thunderbolt and bell) which were used by an eminent lama are more important than an older but inferior or little-used set. Much of the shoddier stuff is actually Nepalese, sold by Tibetans at a handsome profit, but if you know where to look, there are still some very skilled craftsmen to be found. It is a revelation to see something that is well made and not artificially aged; there are more skilled craftsmen in Dharamsala than is apparent from casual inspection, but they work in out-of-the-way private homes for the most part, so you have to live there in order to get to know them. This is particularly true of the jewellers, who are well worth finding. The other shops, with their dark, mysterious-smelling interiors, have already been mentioned.

In a modest way, Dharamsala is quite an attraction for tourists. Some are serious students of Tibetan culture or religion, and return repeatedy, but others are just old-fashioned hippies: just as the Raj retired from Delhi to Simla when the weather grew too hot, the hippies move from Goa to Dharamsala. Some sleep rough, and others hire rooms in private

houses for next to nothing; some of the wealthier ones rent whole houses. Between these two rather predictable extremes, there are many other types of visitor. Inevitably, there are journalists, and even more pseudo-journalists. If every 'journalist' in Dharamsala were published, there would be nothing else in the world's newspapers for a week. There are many, too, who are strictly *sui generis*; and old lady touring India in order to take pictures of sponsored children, then to return to England and raise more sponsorship, or a retired doctor – to be accurate, a *Herr Professor Doktor* – who loves to travel. There are even a few Indian tourists, who stay mostly at the Hotel Bagsu, owned by the Himachal Pradesh Tourist Board. All the other hotels in McLeod Ganj are Tibetan-owned. The Hotel Tibet is owned by the Tibetan Administration, but unfortunately the running of it is very patchy. Nevertheless, the best rooms on the roof are where the better-off Western tourists stay. The rooms on the middle floor are favoured by the modestly affluent, whilst those on the bottom floor are the pits, both colloquially and literally. Places like the Green Hotel and the Rainbow Hotel offer basic but quite respectable accommodation, and there are some strange hybrids such as the Moen Kyi lodge, which caters mostly to long-stay clients who want somewhere clean and decent, but as cheap as reasonably possible. There are rooms to let all over Dharamsala, from five rupees a day to two hundred a day at the time of writing: the standards are comparably widely varied.

Part of the Dhauladur Himalayan spur, seen from the roof of the Hotel Tibet.

At one of the frequent Tibetan demonstrations outside the Chinese embassy in Delhi, an old woman weeps for her country.

Some of the hotels have their own restaurants, but there are others for the more adventurous. The Friends' Corner is Tibetan-run, and one of the best; another is the ominously named Rising Horizon Cafe, and another is the Tibet Memory. Because of the ways in which things have happened, some of these restaurants are owned by quite unlikely bodies: the Tibetan Youth Congress owns one (and a shop) which is a long way from the rather radical political image which it usually has. The TYC (Tibetans are as fond of abbreviations as the British) numbers among its members some fairly elderly youths, many in their thirties or even forties, but it has organised many demonstrations outside the Chinese embassy in Delhi.

After the Administration, and the hoteliers, shop-keepers, and restaurateurs, the other source of income for most people is handicrafts. The jewellers have already been mentioned, but there are also a few tailors (of very varying ability) and a lot of carpet-weavers.

Although few people are aware of Tibetan rugs and carpets,

those who are can hardly sing their praises loudly enough. Deep and luxurious, they are hand-knotted and then trimmed to give a pile which will last for three-quarters of a century on the floor, and centuries if they are used as chair-mats or bed-mats. Anyone who likes a firm bed should try sleeping on wooden boards, covered with a Tibetan rug as a mattress. For real luxury, use two rugs, or a horsehair or flock pad an inch or two thick under the rug. These rugs and carpets are woven to traditional patterns, in brilliant colours, or in more subdued tones better suited to certain types of Western decor. It is even possible to specify your own pattern. All you have to do is send a drawing of the pattern you want, a list of colours (or samples), and the size. It will be woven to your requirements. Some people even have armorial bearings woven into rugs.

The rugs are woven in many places – in the TCV, as already mentioned, in a government-sponsored carpet factory, and in private homes. Carpet-weaving is probably the main cash-earner for the Tibetans, and every settlement has its own carpet factory or factories. Sometimes, the most out-of-the-way settlements produce the best carpets: the settlement at Hunsur, to which we shall return later, makes some of the very finest.

Finally, of course, there are the monks and nuns. No one knows exactly how many monasteries there are in Dharamsala: it is something of a meaningless question, because a single monk may constitute a monastery. This is especially true if he is there as the representative of another monastery which is somewhere else in India.

Although the life of all monasteries follows broadly the same pattern, certain monasteries are noted for particular activities or specialities. In Dharamsala, for example, the Nechung monastery is the home of the State Oracle of Tibet. He is not consulted as often nowadays as he was in Tibet, but he still works from time to time, and is highly respected. The Dalai Lama's own monastery, Phendey Lekshey Ling, traditionally supplied administrators. Many of the great monasteries of Tibet have been re-founded in India, including the triad which were most powerful before the invasion, Sera, Ganden, and Drepung. Sera is at Bylakuppe, and Ganden and Drepung are both in Mundgod; these settlements are scattered around Bangalore in Karnataka state, in south India.

Many Westerners have never met a monk, even from a Christian tradition, and few have any idea of what the monastic life entails. Prayer, at fixed intervals throughout the day, is obviously one aspect: it is salutary to recall that the need to know the times of prayer was one of the main reasons for the development of clocks in the West. There is also what might be called 'religious research', an attempt to understand more fully the mysteries of life, and man's place in the universe. This is done not only from books, but also by meditation and debate. Some monks, though not all, will be assigned tasks outside the monastery, and others will work inside: there are monk tractor-drivers, and monk-mechanics, and monk-electricians, and monk-cooks. Cooking for a monastery of a thousand monks is a time-consuming process, even when the food is as basic as it is, and young monks are often assigned in turn to the kitchens as helpers.

The youth of some of the monks is a most curious phenomenon to Western eyes. The tradition of entering the monastery at a very early age – perhaps six or seven, though more usually ten or twelve – is not as widespread as it was in the old Tibet, but it still happens. The young monks do not seem unhappy, and from time to time one meets children whose dearest desire is to become a monk, but whose parents are restraining them in order to make sure that the vocation is real. I met one boy who was about to enter Sera as a novice; he was eleven years old, and he said that he had wanted to be a monk ever since he was eight. It is hard to understand this attitude if one comes from a completely different culture, but from meeting monks of any age it soon becomes clear that the path they have chosen is by no means as different from everyday life as it might be in the West. The religious impulse in the man in the street is so strong, and the life of the monk so open and

Followers of the monastic life take many forms: a peaceful Abbot in the south; a powerfully-built monk in the north; or as a young novice who could not resist a peek at what was going on. Discipline is at once rigorous and lax: without internal discipline, the external forms are meaningless. Furthermore, the emphasis on debate in Tibetan religious education means that there is little scope for didacticism.

This nun lives in a tiny retreat which is no more than a crack in the rock plastered over with a mud wall – but she invited a monk, a ngakpa, and the author in for tea. She had to carry the water to make it half a mile up the hillside.

down-to-earth, that their lives seem merely to be different aspects of the same thing.

I have concentrated on monks, because there are far fewer nuns. The only major convent is in Dharamsala, though there are solitary nuns in many places. The convent nuns tend to be more isolated than monks, and more formal, but the others live lives very similar to their male counterparts, and have no qualms about talking to men.

Before leaving the religious side of life, it is worth mentioning the ngakpas and the Bonpo. Ngakpas, literally Tantric-rite (*ngak*) practitioners (*-pa*) are sometimes translated as 'sourcerers', but this is very misleading in the Judaeo-Christian tradition. They are not necessarily celibate, nor need they take the conventional monastic vows, but they are far from lone magicians. They are best regarded as the cutting edge of Buddhist mysticism, working in the realms of visions and the supernatural as a matter of course. The path they choose is seen as the fastest road to enlightenment, but also the most dangerous: like a man on a steep and rocky mountain path, they will reach the top faster than the man on the safer road, but the journey requires more effort and more intense concentration – and they will fall further and harder if they miss their footing. They are most emphatically not 'black magicians'; it is said that if any ngakpa works ill against anyone, or even performs some ill-considered action which leads to harm, the harm will return to him multiplied many-fold.

Similarly, the Bonpo are not the ogres that they are sometimes painted. Bon is the old, pre-Buddhist religion of Tibet, and it still has its adherents. It is true that there is a tradition

136

of black Bon, just as there is a tradition of black magic in the Christian church, but it is negligible – about as important as black magic is to Christianity, in fact. To the outsider, Bon and Buddhism may seem almost indistinguishable, because there has been over a thousand years of cross-fertilisation and mutual influence, but the differences in aim and content are the subject of fierce (but still peaceful) argument, even among those who understand the subject far better than I, so it is a minefield into which I will not wander. Even so, it is worth noting that there is little evidence of Bon in Dharamsala, and the Bonpo are found mostly in Solan, about a hundred miles away.

It is important to realise, however, that Little Lhasa is only one settlement, and far from typical at that. Most of the others, scattered across India, are agricultural. There are over three dozen of them, together with a few in Nepal, and although some consist of little more than a single monastery and a few lay people, others are major settlements with populations of several thousand people. By way of example, it is worth looking at just two, Bylakuppe and Hunsur in south India.

In contrast to the nun's spartan quarters is the magnificent interior of this monastery in Clement Town, near Dehra Dun. The great 'gold' statues are actually gilded clay or (as the Lama put it) 'mud'.

Tibetan road gangs built many strategic roads in the Himalayas, near the Tibetan border, where their experience of working at high altitude meant that they could do the work of three or four Indians.

Bylakuppe (pronounced *By-lah-coo-pay*) is the biggest and oldest of the Tibetan agricultural settlements in India. It was founded in 1960, on virgin forest land granted rent-free and exempt from land taxes by the Indian government. The first 666 settlers arrived in mid-December 1960, and began to clear the jungle with the minimum of equipment, and indeed entirely without bulldozers. At first they lived in tents, but the first permanent buildings were of mud-plastered bamboo, and many people still live in such houses today, though the modern camp buildings and the more recent houses are of brick. Clearing the land was back-breaking work, but the settlers were used to this: many had previously been working on road-building in the Himalayas, where the Indian government had been glad to employ them because at those altitudes a Tibetan could do as much work as two or three Indians.

Homes in the south of India tend to be plain concrete boxes, but they are considerably more weatherproof than the Dharamsala shanties. This one is in Hunsur.

A Bylakuppe street market reminiscent of those in Lhasa is held once a week – but there are no bullets for sale here.

In Bylakuppe, a few tens of miles from Hunsur, the great Indian bicycle has made a far greater impact on the Tibetans' lifestyle than it has in mountainous Dharamsala or poverty-stricken Hunsur.

There are still a few of these road-gangs left, and they form an important chapter in the history of Tibetans in exile, but it is a chapter better left unread. Whole families lived in tents by the roadside, and the children who lived – many did not – worked as soon as they were old enough to break and carry stones. From time to time, the memory of those days comes back with unexpected force; when sending my condolences to a friend whose father had just died, I asked our mutual friend whom I had asked to convey my feelings whether the man's mother was still alive. "No," he said, "he lost his mother many years ago, on the road-gangs." To hear this of a man whom I knew only as an urbane, dedicated, and capable administrator was a salutary shock.

On the southern plains of India, even worse than in the mountains, India's hot, wet climate took its toll of the refugees. Tibetan hygiene was always rudimentary, but in the high, thin, dry air of Tibet it was not too important: in the Indian south, it was fatal. They struggled on, however, and planted rice, lentils, oilseed, cotton, coriander, and tobacco; as time progressed, they found that maize was both the most reliable and the most profitable crop, and this remains the staple to this day, so that even the mandala offerings traditionally made with barley or rice are now often made with maize in the south. The problem, as with any one-crop economy, is that they are at the mercy of both market fluctuations and adverse conditions. Moves are afoot to diversify the crop again, but because maize is proven, few are willing to chance their luck on any other crops.

Opposite *Tibetans are inveterate shopkeepers, and their shops usually recapture the jumbled mystery of shops recalled from childhood, even when they are tidy and well-organised.*

The water supply in Bylakuppe is by no means reliable, and these young monks have been sent to fill up every container they can lay their hands on.

In addition to agriculture, the settlers at Bylakuppe also keep dairy cattle and chickens. Strange as it may seem, most of the hens are kept under battery conditions, as egg producers; the sight of all those hens crammed into battery cages may not be pleasant, but most people would prefer it to the sight of a starving child. The dairy cattle are another matter; some are kept in modern byres, but many are kept individually, or in small numbers, by families.

Handicrafts also play an important part in the economy of the settlement. There are carpet factories, one in the Old Camp and one in the New Camp, and an incense factory where the fragrant ingredients are ground together into a paste and then extruded through a die, an altogether more sophisticated form of manufacture than the Indian dipping method. Tibetan incense has a much heavier and rather more

Incense manufacture, using traditional ingredients, is quite a profitable industry in Bylakuppe. The incense is mixed as a paste, extruded through a die, dried on a board, and then bundled for sale.

'churchy' smell than the Indian variety. A surprisingly important industry is the sale of woollen sweaters, traditionally peddled all around India in the winter, which leads to a shortage of handicraft workers during the winter season.

The biggest branch of TCV is also in Bylakuppe. Arranged on lines very similar to those of the Village in Dharamsala, it obviously caters for Tibetan children, but just up the road there is also an Indian government school with both Indian and Tibetan children. Walking through the community, the overall impression is (by Indian standards) one of modest prosperity. The houses are small and cramped, but not impossibly so, and Tibetan hygiene has perforce made enormous steps – even though the water supply is not too reliable. Overall, the two Camps of the settlement provide a home for more than ten thousand refugees.

The Hunsur colony, perhaps two hours' drive from Bylakuppe, is much smaller, newer, and poorer. It was begun at the end of 1971, and at the time of writing contained about 2,500 people living off much poorer land than at the older settlement. There is also a completely different feel to the place: in Bylakuppe, there is a certain complacency, but in Hunsur there is a realistic awareness of the problems which they face, and a strong determination to overcome them. One thing which really brings home the meaning of 'subsistence farming' is the maize crop: they have to borrow from the banks each year in order to buy their seed-corn, and in order to pay off their debts before they become too great, they have to sell the crop as soon as it is in. If they could afford to store their surplus, they could get several times as much for the corn later in the year, when the glut was over; but they cannot afford to do it. What is so frustrating is that the amount of money required is, by Western standards, negligible: less than £25,000, or just over three lakhs of rupees, would free them from the need to borrow, make them self-sufficient, and enable them to build a prosperous base. When you see these people, working so hard, so cheerful and honest, and realise that the whole community could be made affluent for under

A reliable supply of good water is one of Hunsur's few blessings.

Each of these cans contains the day's milk surplus from a single family in Hunsur. The few paise *earned from the sale of half a litre, or a litre, or two litres of milk every day is vital income. The milk in each can is tested by an Indian government inspector to make sure that it is not watered, then measured and entered in the ledger.*

£1 (or just over a dollar) a head, it is impossible to describe the feelings which rise in your heart.

In Hunsur, most cattle are kept either individually or in small co-operatives. Typically, a family will keep one or two cows and retain half the milk for their own use and sell the other half. It is sold on a daily basis, and the queue of people with their little jars and cans of milk drives home yet again what subsistence farming is all about: the maximum that any individual will bring is four or five litres (about a gallon), and many can only bring a litre or two. Then you think again, and realise that this is better than their fellow-countrymen in their own land can expect...

Once again there is a carpet factory, and the carpets woven there are of the finest quality that I have seen from any work-shop: deep, soft, and superbly executed. They are absolutely magnificent. But the settlement cannot afford to advertise, and must go through a middleman, so their profits are no-thing like what they should be. Again and again in Hunsur, I kept thinking: these people deserve better than this.

The same story could be repeated through all the other set-tlements in India, and each could add stories of its own. The magnificent temples of Clement Town, outside Dehra Dun, spring to mind; the Nyingma monastery of Ngedon Gyatsel-ling, the biggest monastery of the Ancient Order in India, with its school full of young monks and its open-handed hospital-ity; the people clustered patiently around the stand-pipe in Chauntra, waiting for the slow dribble of water to fill the big plastic jerry-cans at dawn, because the water would not last all day; the old, old lady spinning wool in Bir, giggling like a schoolgirl because I was taking her picture; the *Ngakpa* at Tso.Pema, the Lotus Lake sacred to Guru Rinpoche, offering us rum and water at seven in the morning, sitting cross-legged behind the low table in his rented room, radiating power. There were tales I have not even begun to tell here, of how the Tibetan communities of Switzerland and Canada have pros-pered, and of how they send money back to the Administration, or of individual Tibetans in America, France, Holland, Japan, and many other countries.

One thing that I can say, though, is that I have made more friends, more quickly, among Tibetans than I have ever done elsewhere in my life; and that when I talk about what Tibetans have done, and what they need, and what they hope for, I often say 'we' and not 'they'. My Tibetan friends sometimes smile, but they do not correct me. I hope that through this book, you have begun to share something of the same feeling.

GLOSSARY

Bardo: 'between-life' state
Bodhisattvas: those who have attained enlightenment but remain manifest for the purpose of teaching
Bod-rGyal-ho: Royal Year
chang: barley beer
Chöd: magical 'cutting' practice
chorten: religious monument, receptacle of mind
chuba: traditional Tibetan dress
de-pon: secular rank
Desi: Prime Minister
Dharma: Buddhist teaching
dorje and *drilbu:* thunderbolt and bell
dri: cow of Tibetan cattle
dung-chen: great horn
dzongs: administrative centres (literally 'fortress')
Gelong: final vows for Tibetan monks
Getsul: preliminary vows of Tibetan monks
Gyalyum Chhenmo: Great Mother (of Dalai Lama)
Hinayana: the Lesser Vehicle (in Buddhist teaching)
jaa: a medicament (poultice for sprains)
katags: ceremonial scarves
khabse: home-made fried biscuits

khel: measure of weight (about 13 kg)
Lha: gods
Lhamo: goddesses; Folk Opera
Losar: Tibetan New Year
lung-gom: long-distance runners
Madayana: the Greater Vehicle (in Buddhist teaching)
mani: stones bearing sacred inscriptions
Mimang Tsogdu: 'People's Movement'
ngakpas: Tantric practitioners
Nyingmapa: Ancient Order (of Buddhists)
Rinchen Gyan-cha: Precious Ornaments
rtogs.lden: body-breakers
Sangha: community of monks
shunyata: voidness
Sonam-Palzom: coriander (also a girl's name)
thamzing: mutual self-criticism
thangkas: religious scroll paintings
Therevada School of Buddhism: the Way of the Elders
Trikor Chuksum: the 13 myriarchies
tsampa: ground roast barley
Vajrayana: Thunderbolt path
Yab-shi: 'Royal Family'
yak: bull of Tibetan cattle

POSTSCRIPT - PHOTOGRAPHY

Many of the photographs in this book are derived from an incredible range of sources, and no technical information whatsoever is available. Photographers may however be interested in the following information about the specially-shot material:

Roger Hicks uses mainly rangefinder Leicas – M2s and an M4-P – with 21mm f/2.8, 35mm f/1.4 and 90mm f/2 lenses. The large format pictures in this book were mostly taken with Linhofs, a Technika 70 and a Super Technika IV, both 6x9cm models with 6x7cm rollfilm backs.

Frances Schultz used mainly Nikkormats, with the following lenses: 24mm f/2.8 and 50mm f/1.2 Nikkors, and 90mm f/2.5 and 200mm f/3 Vivitar Series Ones. She also used a Mamiya 645 kindly supplied by the makers, with 35mm f/3.5, 80mm f/1.9, and 150mm f/3.5 lenses.

The vast majority of 35mm colour is on Kodachrome 64, with the 120 colour on Ektachrome 64. The main black-and-white film stocks used were Ilford FP4 and HP5. Metering was by Weston Masters.

The main technical problems were keeping dust out of the cameras and equipment – self-sealing plastic bags, inside Zero Halliburton cases, took care of that – and keeping the colour filmstocks from 'cooking'. Wherever possible, we kept the film in a refrigerator; Kodachrome's extraordinary resistance to maltreatment was also a blessing. As ever in this sort of photography, the logistical problems of getting to our locations and actually carrying the equipment were more important than the exact type of camera used – though no cameras could have behaved more reliably than the ones which we used. Only the Mamiya was battery dependent, and although we carried three spare batteries, we never needed to change one unexpectedly, or indeed at all, in the course of our travels.

PHOTO CREDITS

Where two names are given the first is the name of the institution supplying the picture or material, the second is the name of the photographer.

Collection of H.H. the Dalai Lama: 14, 15, *top*, 25, 31, 34, 40, 41, 42, 45, 46, 47 *bottom*, 48 *top*, 49, 50, 51, 52 *top*, 53, 54, 55, 57, 59 *bottom*, 65, 67, 68, 70 *top*, 73, 89

Alexandra David-Neel Collection: 13, 15 *bottom*, 23 *bottom*, 30, 47 *top*

Mrs Pema Gyalpo: 16, 79, 80, 83

Collection of Mrs Pema Gyalpo: 74, 78 *top*, 81, 84, 100 *top*

Hicks: *frontispiece*, 12, 19 *top*, 21, 37 *bottom*, 48 *bottom*, 52 *bottom*, 82 *top*, 104, 105, 106, 108, 110, 113, 114, 115, 117, 118, 119, 120, 121 *bottom*, 122, 123 *top right*, 123 *bottom*, 124, 125, 126 *top*, 127, 128, 130, 132, 134, 135, 136 *top*, 137, 138 *top*, 139, 140, 141 *bottom*, 142, 144, 146, 147, 148, 149, 151, 152, 153 *top*, 154, 155, 156, 157

Hicks/Schultz: 102, 109

Information Office: 17 *bottom*, 38, 62, 78 *bottom*, 88, 90, 100 *bottom*, 107, 111, 112, 131 *top*, 153 *bottom*

Kashag: 77 *top*, 85, 91, 92, 94, 95, 98 *bottom*

LTWA: 17, 28, 36, 64, 70 *bottom*, 72 *bottom*

LTWA / Hicks: 23 *top*, 27

The Newark Museum: 59 *top*

Office of His Holiness, New York: 76, 77 *top*, 82 *bottom*, 98 *top*, 101

George Patterson: 86, 87, 97, 136 *bottom*

Schultz: 32, 109 *top*, 121 *top*, 123 *top left*, 131 *bottom*, 136 *bottom*, 138 *bottom*

Tibetan Children's Village Collection: 150

Vijender Tyagi; courtesy *Tibetan Review*: 143

Volkerkundermuseum Zurich: 29, 37 *top*

Volkerkundermuseum Zurich/Aufschnaiter: 66, 71, 196

Volkerkundermuseum Zurich/Harrer: 33, 35, 44, 58, 69, 72 *top*

Kim Yeshi: 61